Think
Through
History

Meetings of Minds:

Islamic encounters c. 570 to 1750

Jamie Byrom

Christine Counsell

Michael Riley

PEARSON

Longman

Meetings of Minds:
Islamic Encounters c. 570-1750

This book tells some fascinating stories of a remarkable religion and its encounters with the wider world. It begins long ago in the land of the Arab peoples – the ancient land of Arabia.

Around 570 AD, the Arabs lived in their separate tribes, full of differences and disputes. They were surrounded by three vast and powerful **empires**: the **Sasanians**, the **Byzantines** and the **Abyssinians**.

The Sasanians and Byzantines had no plans to conquer Arabia. They were happy just to control its edges to the north and west. They saw no need to conquer the Arabs. What would be the point?

Surely nothing would ever unite these Arabs?

Surely the Arabs would never challenge the ancient Sasanian, Byzantine and Abyssinian empires?

Surely nothing of any real strength or lasting value could come from the deserts of Arabia… could it?

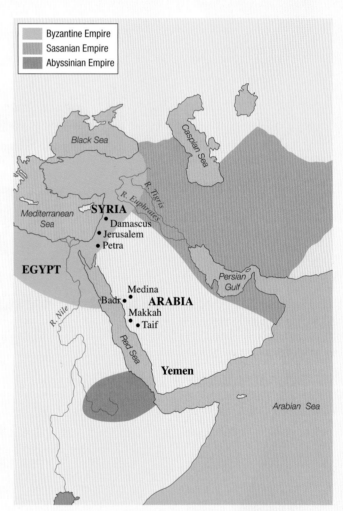

A map showing Arabia and the surrounding empires c. 570 AD

500	600	700	800	900	1000

c. 570 Birth of Muhammad

632 Death of Muhammad

661 Umayyad clan takes control of Islam

747 Abbasids take power from Umayyads

750 Muslim lands reached from Spain to India

c. 800 House of Wisdom established in Baghdad

1000 Cordoba's mosque completed

1071 Seljuk Turks attack Byzantine Empi

1099 Christian Crusaders (Franks) capture Jerusalem

Your enquiries

1 The sacred city

How did the people of Makkah see their world?   4

2 Alarmed and inspired in Arabia

What did people make of Muhammad's message?   12

3 Problems, problems

What difficulties did Muslims face after Muhammad?   20

4 So far, so fast

Why did Islam spread?   25

5 "All the treasures of the world"

What was so special about Baghdad?   32

6 A place to pray

What does the story of Cordoba reveal?   42

7 Threats from beyond

How can we know what Muslims thought of Crusaders and invaders?   54

8 "With my own eyes"

How can we picture the world of Ibn Battuta?   64

9 The rose and its thorns

How did the Ottoman sultans show their power?   74

10 Three Toms' travels

What did English people think about the Islamic world 1550-1750?   84

1100	1200	1300	1400	1500	1600	1700

1187 Saladin regains Jerusalem

1258 Mongols destroy Baghdad

c. 1260-1300 Mamluks defeat Mongols and Franks

1346 Ibn Battuta reaches China

1453 Ottomans capture Christian city of Constantinople

1492 Christians remove last Muslim ruler in Spain

1599 Elizabeth I seeks trade agreement with Ottomans

1654 Taj Mahal built

1725 Thomas Pellow captured by Barbary corsairs

The sacred city

How did the people of Makkah see their world?

Imagine an ancient city in the middle of a desert. Picture the city just before dawn. Twenty thousand people are sleeping.

Imagine our city as it starts to wake. As the sun appears above the mountains, what will we see?

The early light reveals hundreds of flat rooftops. Soon, we make out the shapes of fine stone houses, some simple wooden huts and tents made of black goats' hair.

As sunlight floods across roads and alleyways, we see men asleep by doorways. (It was so hot last night that they slept outside in the desert breeze.) Women light fires in clay ovens, children carry water, mules pad softly through sandy streets.

We are looking at the city of Makkah, the sacred city of Arabia, in the year 570.

On the edge of the city are the camel stables of great merchants. Imagine the camels walking in lines, called **caravans**, along one of the four roads:

- The road to the northeast stretches hundreds of miles across the deserts of central Arabia to the great **Sasanian Empire**.
- The road to the north leads across the Syrian desert towards the markets of Damascus. This is a gateway into the vast **Byzantine Empire**: the eastern part of the old Roman Empire. Christianity is the main religion there.
- The western road leads to the Red Sea. Across this sea are the Christian lands of Egypt and Abyssinia.
- The southern road reaches out to the perfume markets of the Yemen.

Right now, Makkah is busy. This is the time of pilgrimage. It feels like a big fair or festival. **Bedouin tribes** camp round the city. Traders sell perfumes from eastern Africa, rich cloths and silks from Egypt or China and slaves from everywhere.

The **pilgrims** have come to a holy city. Already this morning, a few pilgrims are moving around a large, black, square temple called the **Kaaba**. Around the Kaaba are over 300 holy objects made of stone or wood. Some are Christian or Jewish. (They say there is an image of the Virgin Mary and even a portrait of Abraham.) But most are **idols** of the **pagan** gods. The Arabs worship gods and spirits that live in stones, trees and wells.

So this city is
... not just a stopping point for the camel caravans of Arabia,
...not just a market full of traders,
... not just home to 20,000 people.
It is a sacred place.

Now imagine a scene in the city. A messenger runs to the house of a rich merchant – an elderly leader of the powerful **Quraysh** tribe. This tribe controls the city and its trade. The messenger has come from the merchant's daughter-in-law, Aminah. Breathless from running, he is shouting:

"Come to Aminah's house! She has a son!"

The elderly merchant hurries to Aminah's house. He will have to be father to the new child because his son, Aminah's husband, is dead.

The old man carries his new grandson to the Kaaba. There, he thanks God for the child. The baby will be called Muhammad.

Your enquiry

This city is the setting for an extraordinary story. It is the story of a person, Muhammad, and it is the story of the birth of a new religion, Islam.

For this story to make sense, we need to understand the hearts and minds of the people of Muhammad's world, both in the city of Makkah and all around it.

You are going to use the story of Muhammad's early life to work out the ideas of these people. What was important to them? What did they fear? You will make a 'people collage' to show these ideas.

Growing up with the Bedouin

When Muhammad was a few days old, some Bedouin came to Makkah from their grazing lands. While the men were busy in the animal markets, the Bedouin women set off on donkeys to visit the wealthy houses of the Quraysh tribe. They asked the women of the Quraysh if there were any newborn children who they could foster and feed with their own milk. This was the custom: the Bedouin women would receive no money, but when they returned the children, they would expect a gift.

A Bedouin woman called Halimah chose to foster Aminah's new son. She took him back into the desert with her own people.

There are many stories about Muhammad as a small boy. We will never know whether some are true or not. What we do know is that he lived in the desert with his foster mother, Halimah. This was the life of a **nomad** – a life on the move. It was a simple life, lived in harsh conditions, with hardly any personal possessions.

The young Muhammad lived in one of the clan's tents, sharing one side with the women and children. He would have learned about hospitality towards strangers and about helping the poor and sick, widows and orphans. He would have listened to poems about love, war and history, for which the Bedouin were famous. He would have learned about the ancient religion of Arabia, the sacred places, the kind spirits and the frightening **jinn**.

Return to the family

Muhammad returned to his mother when he was about six. She took him to see his relatives who lived a few days' camel-ride away. One story says that Muhammad and his mother made kites together. They flew them in the desert winds.

But Muhammad was not to know his mother for long. Aminah was ill. Before they had returned home, she was dead.

Muhammad's grandfather took care of him. But his grandfather was now old and ill. Soon he, too, was dead.

So when Muhammad was about eight years old, he passed into the care of his uncle, the merchant, Abu Talib.

Learning camel management

Muhammad was part of the powerful Quraysh tribe, but he was not rich. His widowed mother had just five camels and one slave. Muhammad would have to make his own wealth. He would have to learn about trade. His uncle, Abu Talib, prepared him well.

First, young boys learned to care for sheep and goats. Only then could they learn to care for the most important animal in the Arab world, the camel. A camel was everything. Without one, a man was nothing. He could be neither a warrior nor a merchant. A camel could buy a wife or pay off the blood guilt of a murder. A camel was a sign that you were somebody. (In any love poem of ancient Arabia, you have to check whether the poet is praising a lover or a camel!)

Muhammad would have spent years learning about camels: where to graze them, how to rest them, where to find water. He had to stop his camels from grazing on the pastures of unfriendly tribes. The young Muhammad also learned about trade. Some stories say that he joined his uncle, Abu Talib, on a trading caravan to Syria when he was only nine.

STEP 1

Write some sentences about what people in Muhammad's world believed, thought, knew, hoped or feared. These are your 'ideas sentences'. Do not start with 'People...' or 'They...'. **Be precise!** For example,

- **Bedouin tribes people believed...**
- **Wealthy families in Makkah were happy to...**
- **Bedouin children would learn...**
- **Traders knew about...**
- **Pilgrims thought...**

Your sentences will be suggestions. As you learn more, you can revise them.

The world of Muhammad

Muhammad's world was many worlds:

A world of clans and tribes

No kings, emperors or governors ruled the pagan tribes of Arabia. There were no judges or law courts. Instead there were families, clans and tribes. About a hundred families made a **clan**. Above the clan was the tribe. Each clan had rights over wells and pastures. It fought and travelled together. A group of respected men would meet to make important decisions.

We are loyal to our clan and loyal to our tribe

Clan   *Clan*   *Clan*

Loyalty to your clan was a great virtue. Revenge was a duty. The only protection against murder was the **blood feud**, when a clan would avenge a death by killing a man from the murderer's clan. Blood feuds went on for generations. Without protection from clan and tribe, no-one was safe.

Not everyone liked this system. This story from when Muhammad was young shows that *some* people in Makkah wanted things to be different:

A powerful Quraysh merchant took the goods of a Yemeni merchant without paying for them. He knew he could get away with it. His clan would protect him. A group of men decided that this was wrong. They formed a brotherhood called 'lovers of justice'. They poured water over the Kaaba, drank from it and swore loyalty to each other. Such men wanted fairness and justice to be *more important* than loyalty to the clan. They made sure the Yemeni merchant was paid for his goods.

Think

- Why would many Arabs see the ideas of the 'lovers of justice' as dangerous or wrong?

A world of different religions

Through the caravan trade, pagan Arabs met Christians and Jews who lived in Syria, Egypt and Abyssinia. Muhammad might have heard Christian and Jewish stories told by the campfires on the long caravan journeys across the desert.

Muhammad's uncle, Abu Talib, had trading links with the Christians of Abyssinia. Muhammad himself may have heard Christian preachers on his travels. There were also Jewish communities in Arabia. Many pagan Arabs knew about Jewish beliefs and holy sites.

A world of poems

Arabia was full of poets. Arabs loved to listen to stories in verse. Most poets did not read or write. At the annual fairs, hundreds gathered to listen to poets recite verses from memory. Poets composed verses in praise of brave young warriors, important ancestors, the beauty of the desert or the beauty of a loved one (...or of a camel).

Poems kept alive the memory of ancestors. That was the only 'afterlife' that most pagan Arabs wanted. Life after death was for weak people, slaves and grieving widows. A brave Arab was expected to make the most of love and glory in *this* life. If the proud men of the Quraysh started believing in life after death, the Bedouin would just laugh at them!

> How could the dry old bones in the sand come back to life? Ridiculous idea!

A world of stories about a glorious past

To travel north to Syria was to travel through the history of Arabia. The camel caravans passed through ruins of ancient cities like Petra. Roman armies had destroyed these once great cities. The caravan trail led through many remains of old Arab cultures and empires. Some Arabs saw the destruction of their glorious cities as God's judgement on them.

The GREAT CITY of PETRA was here

A world of hopes and longings

Not all pagan Arabs were happy with worshipping special stones and lots of gods. There were some Arabs who believed in one god. They were known as '**Hanifs**'. These Arabs did not become Jews or Christians, but they made links between their own God, Allah, and the Jewish and Christian belief in one God. They were searching for something, but they were not sure what.

The Hanifs sometimes left noisy, crowded Makkah and camped in the desert or mountains where they could pray and think.

> If only we worshipped one God...

> If only we could live in a better way...

> If only...

STEP 2

Now use this section to work out more ideas that Arab people held. Write some more 'ideas sentences'.

Makkah's precious trade

The merchants of Makkah were proud of their rich trade. Imagine the different goods the young Muhammad might have seen pass through the city:

- *grapes*, *melons* and *cucumbers* from the nearby city of Taif.
- *sheep*, *goats*, *horses* and *camels*, reared in the desert and exchanged for *dates*, *grain* and *textiles* grown in the fertile land around oases.
- *skins* made into leather bottles, leather bags and leather bridles.
- *frankincense* burned by Christians, Jews and pagans in their shrines and at festivals, and the expensive, fragrant oil known as *myrrh*.

But the merchants of Makkah could never take this trade for granted. Control of the caravan trade might not last forever. Makkah's greatness might not last forever. Even her ruling tribes might not last forever. Just recently Makkah had nearly lost everything…

Around the time Muhammad was born, the Abyssinians nearly attacked Makkah. The Abyssinian army was terrifying because it included an elephant! Luckily for Makkah, the army fell ill with a plague and fled home. Long afterwards, people in Makkah would have told their children this story. They even called 570 'the Year of the Elephant'.

So Muhammad grew up in a proud city, a city that knew danger. This was a city that had to protect its people and protect its precious trade.

A beloved wife

By the time Muhammad was a young merchant, stories had spread about how honest he was. Some people seem to have called him al-Amin, 'the trusted one'.

A rich widow, Khadijah, wanted to know if he was as trustworthy and honourable as she had heard. Khadijah sent her servant to watch Muhammad on a trading caravan to Syria. When the servant gave a good report, Khadijah sent a matchmaker to ask if Muhammad was interested in marriage. He said that he was.

Their closest male relatives would have planned their engagement. Muhammad probably made an offer of about 20 camels. When this was accepted, Muhammad and Khadijah were free to marry.

Khadijah was wealthy. Muhammad carried on trading, but he was now well-off. He gave money to the poor. There are stories about the generous gifts he gave to his foster mother, Halimah, whenever her Bedouin clan passed through Makkah. Once Khadijah gave Halimah a camel and a herd of 40 sheep.

Khadijah and Muhammad had six children: four girls and two boys. The girls lived and the boys died.

STEP 3

Write more sentences about the ideas of people in Makkah. For example:

- **Merchants probably feared…**
- **Some Arab women…**
- **Christians, Jews and pagans valued…**

Thinking your enquiry through

It is time to make your 'people collage'. It will show what was on the minds of people in Muhammad's time. This is what good historians do: they try to understand the way people in the past saw their world.

Start by making a collection of large outline shapes to represent different kinds of people in Muhammad's world. We have shown you an example below – but yours will be much bigger. Do NOT include Muhammad in your collage.

Above the collage, write the heading **"How the people of Makkah saw their world"**.

Fill the space above the people's heads with the 'ideas sentences' that you made in each Step. Check that your sentences include some ancient Arab ideas about:

- life, death and religion
- good or proper behaviour
- Arabia's past or future
- being weak and being strong
- useful possessions
- justice and fairness.

Draw arrows from each of the ideas sentences down to the heads. This will show that the ideas were **on the minds** of different people in ancient Arabia.

How the people of Makkah saw their world

Alarmed and inspired in Arabia

What did people make of Muhammad's message?

One night, in the year 610, Muhammad was sleeping in a cave on Mount Hira. He woke suddenly to hear the command:

"Recite!"

What could this mean? Muhammad was not like the poets with verses in their heads, nor could he read. So what could he recite? Then more words came:

Muhammad was shaken. Could this really be from God? He left his cave and climbed higher. As he climbed, he saw an angel so big that it filled the whole sky.

Muhammad staggered back to the cave. He told Khadijah his story.

> "Recite! In the name of the Lord your God, who created man from a drop of blood. Recite! The Lord your God, the Most Bountiful One, has taught man to use the pen – taught man what he did not know".

The Koran, Sura 1.

This is a story from Muslim tradition. Historians cannot be sure of the exact facts of such a story, but it is still important in our study of history. Whatever happened that night, it was a turning point. It would change everything.

Your enquiry

You are going to work out why different people in Arabia were alarmed or inspired by what Muhammad said and did. At the end of this enquiry, you will bring to life for a few seconds a person who was alarmed or inspired, all those years ago.

To do this, you need to know the ideas that people already held, so keep your work from Enquiry 1 handy. Remember, you are not working out whether YOU are alarmed or inspired *now*! Think about how people **at the time** would have reacted.

Sharing the messages

Surrender to God!

Muhammad received many more messages. At first, Muhammad shared the messages with very few people. These were the first **Muslims**. They all believed that the messages were **revelations** from God. These first Muslims included his cousin, Ali, and the merchant, Abu Bakr. Together, this little group practised the new religion of **Islam**. Islam means 'surrender'. When they prayed, the Muslims showed surrender to God by kneeling and bowing. Muhammad also taught them:

- there is only one God, **Allah**
- everyone should submit to the will of God
- believers will be rewarded in Paradise
- all believers are equal before God.

Muhammad taught his followers to:

- give thanks to God (not to other gods or spirits)
- care for orphans, the poor, widows and the weak
- pray at regular times and wash before praying
- live a simple life
- fast (to go without food at certain times).

Think

- Which of Muhammad's teachings do you think **alarmed** the proud merchants of the **Quraysh**?

Silence and scorn

After about five years, Muhammad began to preach to more people. On one occasion, he invited leaders of his clan to dine with him. At the dinner, the guests were puzzled. Muhammad did not slaughter a camel or some nice fat sheep. Instead of a fine feast, he shared a simple meal. Then he spoke about God. There was stony silence. Some clansmen thought it was all a big joke and left laughing.

One thing his clansmen would have found shocking was the way Muhammad talked about prayer. These men normally did deals with the gods. They carried out blood sacrifices in return for help. They poured wine onto altars and expected the gods to protect them. But **surrendering** to God? Getting close to God? Bowing meekly? This was the behaviour of weaklings!

When Muhammad said that worshipping idols was wrong, this really was too much. It was an attack on the ancient religion! What would happen to the **pilgrim** trade if the **idols** around the **Kaaba** disappeared? And what on earth would the **Bedouin** think?

From the various stories that have come down to us, one thing seems clear: things now began to get very difficult for the Muslims. The leaders of Muhammad's clan decided that Muhammad was not just a nuisance, he was a danger.

Violence and fear

A group of leading Quraysh approached Muhammad's uncle, Abu Talib. They asked him to remove the protection of the clan from Muhammad:

"Your nephew has cursed our gods, insulted our religion, mocked our way of life… You must let us rid you of him."

But although Abu Talib was not a Muslim, he would not let the clan give up his nephew. Blood loyalty to family came first. He said to Muhammad, "By God I will not give you up".

So the men of the Quraysh had to find other ways to challenge Muhammad. One uncle, Abu Jahl, was devoted to the old gods. He could not hurt Muhammad, but he encouraged violence against Muhammad's followers. Muhammad was safe, but his followers were not:

- Gangs beat up or tortured any slaves who were Muslims.
- Poor Muslims in less powerful tribes and clans were beaten up.
- More powerful Muslims (those protected by their clans) were scorned for betraying their family and the clan's good name.

By 618, neither the Muslims, nor Muhammad's clan, nor anyone who continued to protect Muhammad could marry, trade, join a caravan or even buy food in the markets of Makkah.

But the Muslims did not give up.

Muhammad sent some Muslims far away to safety in Abyssinia. The rest lived together in the streets around Abu Talib's house. There the Muslims' courage impressed others. Gradually the idea that God was both mighty and forgiving began to appeal to people. Through the beauty of their language, the messages that Muhammad received began to work their way into hearts and minds. Many more converts were made.

Then tragedy struck:

Tragedy 1: In 619, Khadijah died. Afterwards Muhammad took more wives, but none could ever replace Khadijah.

Tragedy 2: Muhammad's uncle, Abu Talib, died.

Think

- Why would Abu Talib's death be a disaster for Muhammad?

STEP

Jot down your ideas about why different people were alarmed or inspired by Muhammad's teachings. Make two headings:

alarmed   inspired

14

From suffering to safety

Things changed immediately without the protection of a clan leader:

Dirt was thrown in Muhammad's face.

An excrement-covered sheep's womb was flung over him.

Rotten animals were hurled into his courtyard.

Muhammad desperately needed somewhere safe. He tried the nearby city of Taif, but a jeering crowd chased him away. He tried his mother's clan, but they were too frightened of the Quraysh to shelter him.

Then, in 620, came hope. As usual, Muhammad preached to the pilgrims in Makkah. As usual, the Bedouin heckled, laughed and shouted him down, especially when he attacked idols. But this year, six pilgrims listened. They were from Yathrib, a date-growing area around an oasis, about 400 kilometres to the north.

In 621, 12 Muslim converts came from Yathrib. Muhammad sent a trusted Muslim back with them to teach them how to pray. In 622, the number of Muslims in Yathrib grew again. At a secret meeting by moonlight, a leader from Yathrib made this promise to Muhammad:

"We will protect you as we protect our wives and children. Accept our allegiance, O Messenger of God, for we are men of war, possessed of arms".

During that year, the Muslims began to make their way north to Yathrib.

But Muhammad was still not safe. His uncle, Abu Jahl was planning to murder him.

Abu Jahl's plan involved one brave, young warrior from each clan. Together, each would plunge his sword into Muhammad. This would protect their clans from vengeance as it would be impossible to take revenge on all the clans at once. The men surrounded Muhammad's house and waited. They waited in vain. Muhammad's cousin, Ali slept in Muhammad's bed to fool them, and Muhammad and Abu Bakr slipped out.

The leaders of the Quraysh offered one hundred camels to anyone who could find Muhammad. The hills crawled with Bedouin spies. But Muhammad and Abu Bakr tricked them by riding in the wrong direction, southwest to the Red Sea. Only after many days did they ride up the coast towards Yathrib.

A home in Medina

About five kilometres south of Yathrib, the Muslim refugees stare towards the south.

A fearful silence has fallen. He should be here by now. The afternoon heat from the black rocks at the southern tip of the oasis is intense. In this heat they would normally be resting, but no-one can sleep.

One refugee thinks he can see something. Tiny figures come into view. "He is here!"

As Muhammad and Abu Bakr advance, local villagers, herdsmen, women and slaves all join the last bit of the journey. Children dance in circles. By a grove of palms, a clan of Bedouin joins them in prayers.

The exhausted Muhammad now had quite a problem. Every village in Yathrib wanted him to live with them, so Muhammad let his camel wander where it wanted. The camel wandered through the sandy alleys, past the mud and stone houses, through the allotments and orchards. Eventually, it came to a stop in a yard by an old shed for storing dates. Muhammad paid the owners for the yard. This would be home.

The journey north became known as The **Hejira**. Yathrib would soon be known as Madinat al-Nabi (the City of the Prophet) or Madinah al-Munawarra (Enlightened City). We will call it Medina. Muhammad built a Muslim community in Medina. An open-air prayer hall, shaded by palm trees, became the first **mosque**. A freed slave, Bilal, called the Muslims to prayer from a rooftop.

Stories spread about how Muhammad lived. People heard that he visited the sick, helped servants with their work and would never allow a seat to be reserved for him. He refused to wear luxurious clothes. One of Muhammad's prayers was,

"O Lord! Keep me a poor man, let me die poor and raise me amongst the poor".

Muhammad had many wives. His favourite wife, Aisha, was Abu Bakr's daughter. Muhammad taught that women should be honoured and cared for. He condemned the practice of leaving baby girls to die.

STEP 2

Jot down more ideas about why different people might have been alarmed or inspired.

War

The people of Makkah, especially the Quraysh, did all they could to make things difficult for Medina. Soon Muhammad was preparing for war with Makkah. For Muhammad, it seems that this war was part of the struggle to help God's word survive.

Think

- What other reasons might the Muslims have had for fighting Makkah?

These views of Makkah (right) and Medina (left) are from a nineteenth century Ottoman book

Muhammad knew exactly where to create problems for Makkah – the **caravans**. In early 624, Muslim spies reported that the Syrian caravan of 2,500 camels was returning to Makkah. Muhammad gathered 350 warriors and rode out to meet the caravan at the wells of Badr.

But the Quraysh had spies too. They spotted date stones in some camel dung. This meant that camels from Medina were in the area, so the Quraysh diverted their caravan away. When the Muslims arrived at Badr, they did not the meet the caravan. They met a thousand-strong army from Makkah. They were outnumbered, three to one.

Accounts of the battle describe it as fierce. It seems that the Muslims' discipline and passion took the Makkans by surprise: the Makkans were defeated.

In one story about the battle, Abu Jahl found himself at the mercy of a young Muslim shepherd who he had once publicly beaten in the face. As the shepherd's sword sliced his head from his shoulders, Abu Jahl is said to have cried,

"You have climbed high indeed, little shepherd!".

More struggles

There were other battles: in one the Muslims lost and Muhammad was wounded. In another, the Makkan army tried to besiege Medina, but Muhammad found an engineer who built a huge ditch that the Makkans could not cross.

It seems that the Muslims also came into conflict with two of the many Jewish Arab tribes around Medina. Muhammad confiscated their property, but they went on to support the Quraysh. When a third tribe rebelled, Muslim sources tell us that the rules of tribal warfare were applied: all the men in the tribe were beheaded and the women and children were made slaves. As far as we know, other Jewish Arab tribes lived peacefully with the first Muslims. It is certainly likely that they met and traded with each other.

Truce with Makkah

In 628, Muhammad decided to go to Makkah, but not as a warrior. He decided to go as a pilgrim.

As he approached Makkah at the head of a band of followers dressed in pilgrims' clothes, the Quraysh rushed out to stop him. But Muhammad managed to negotiate a truce. The leaders of the Quraysh allowed Muhammad to make the pilgrimage the following year in 629.

Many Muslims were unhappy with the truce. The Bedouin thought Muhammad should be marching into Makkah and defeating it, not negotiating permission to be a pilgrim, next year!

Think

● Why do you think that the Bedouin were so disappointed in Muhammad's truce?

After this, Muhammad had to rebuild the support of his followers. He gradually won their support once more. He sat under an acacia tree and, one by one, his followers took his hand and swore a beautiful oath.

We cannot be certain of the words of the oath, but one story puts it like this:

"O Messenger of God, I pledge my allegiance to that which is in your soul."

Return to Makkah

It is spring in 629. The Quraysh look down from the hills around their city. They watch as 2,000 Muslims approach. Muhammad is leading the pilgrims to Makkah.

The Quraysh have agreed to leave the city for three days to allow the Muslims to visit the Kaaba. Thousands of eyes watch from the hills. As he approaches, Muhammad bares his right shoulder. Behind him, every Muslim does the same.

Muhammad rides his camel to the Kaaba. He dismounts and makes seven circles around it.

Muslim pilgrims still observe the custom of baring right shoulders

At noon, Bilal makes the call to prayer. The Muslims pour into the courtyard.

The Makkans see the discipline of the Muslims. They see the Muslims treat the sacred Kaaba with respect. They see how important Makkah is in Muslim prayers. Some Makkans, even powerful military leaders from the Quraysh, make a big decision: they convert to Islam.

Think

- Think of other reasons why people in Makkah might have changed their minds when they saw the Muslims.

The following year, in 630, Muhammad marched to Makkah with 10,000 men. It was a peaceful takeover. Muhammad pardoned many people.

Arriving at the Kaaba, he picked up the idols. One by one, he smashed them to the ground.

STEP 3

Now complete your lists: 'alarmed' and 'inspired'.

Thinking your enquiry through

You will now bring one person from seventh-century Arabia back to life.

- **Decide who you will be.**

- **Choose a year between 610 and 630.**

- **Work out whether you would have been alarmed or inspired by Muhammad's teaching. (Or perhaps your character was at first alarmed and later inspired!)**

- **Make a frozen pose, suggesting the kind of person you are. (Are you picking dates? leading a camel? fixing a tent?)**

- **On your teacher's command, come alive. In just fifteen seconds, explain when, how and why your character was alarmed or inspired by Muhammad's message.**

Problems, problems ③

What difficulties did Muslims face after Muhammad?

It is the year 632. It is two years since Muhammad led the **Muslims** to Makkah and smashed the idols in the **Kaaba**. Muslims now control the whole of western Arabia.

But the Muslims of Medina are afraid. Muhammad is ill. He has terrible headaches and a high fever. No one has seen him for days. He is resting in Aisha's room next to the courtyard of the **mosque**. Everyone worries. Everyone wonders, 'Is the Messenger dying? Is he dead?'

Today is Friday. Abu Bakr, Muhammad's father-in-law, is leading morning prayers. Suddenly a whisper spreads through the mosque, "He is here!"

The worshippers look towards the entrance of the mosque. Yes, it is him. They recognise the familiar face, the shining eyes, the long black hair twisted with grey. He watches as his followers pray to **Allah** in the way that he taught them.

Soon, Muhammad returns to Aisha's room. He collapses. Aisha cradles his head but she feels it grow heavy. Muhammad's eyelids flicker, then close.

Your enquiry

After Muhammad, the Muslims faced many problems. Historians are still trying to work out what exactly these problems were and how people saw them at the time. Sometimes, all historians can do is ask good questions! Asking historical questions is important and difficult work. At the end of this enquiry you will make your own 'Little Book of Questions' to help an historian.

Finding a leader?

When Muhammad died, the Muslims needed a new leader:

What shall we do now?

Who will answer our questions about what is right and what is true?

What power should a new leader have?

Who should choose him?

He should be a member of Muhammad's family…

NO! – but he *must* be a member of the **Quraysh**.

The Quraysh are too powerful!

We think he should be a strong fighter…

What's important is that he is close to God.

The Muslims made Abu Bakr their first leader. They called him a **caliph**. Caliph means '**successor**' or 'deputy'. Caliphs did not take on Muhammad's role as Messenger of God. They were just leaders of the Muslim community. The first four caliphs are sometimes called the 'rightly-guided caliphs'.

It is hard to be sure of exact facts about these four men. Many accounts were written decades later. Some details historians are **certain** about. Others we should be **very cautious** about!

Abu Bakr 632-634

Abu Bakr was Aisha's father. Now an old man, he calmed the Muslims after Muhammad's death. Abu Bakr was determined to show that **Islam** had not died with Muhammad. He was determined to carry on uniting all Arabs under Islam. This meant fighting battles.

Abu Bakr also began to send Muslim armies beyond Arabia, into the **Sasanian** and **Byzantine empires**.

Think

● Now read about the four caliphs. As you read, see if you can work out the problems that each one had to solve.

Umar 634-644

Sources describe Umar as tall with big muscles, a bald head and a fiery temper. He was a skilled fighter who spread Islam far outside Arabia. A great organiser, Umar appointed governors of the new Muslim lands, with treasurers, tax collectors, surveyors and judges to help them. Umar even created a system of payments to poor children.

Umar liked speaking in public and mixing with the public. He used to go shopping in the markets of Medina. One day, a man who had been made a slave twice – once by the Byzantines and once by Muslim Arabs – walked up to Umar and stabbed him to death.

Uthman 644-656

Muslim sources honour Uthman for a great achievement. Uthman made sure that all the revelations Muhammad had from God were gathered into one holy book called the **Quran**.

Uthman's enemies, however, did not like the way he led the Muslims. They said he favoured his own clan – the **Umayya**. Eventually, some Muslim rebels stabbed Uthman. One story says that Uthman fell onto his Quran, his blood soaking into its pages.

Ali 656-661

Ali was Muhammad's cousin. He had been married to Fatima, Muhammad's daughter. Ali is usually described as bald and stocky with a long white beard.

Some Muslims had wanted Ali to be caliph all along. They said that he was the right person to keep Muhammad's teachings alive. This was partly because Ali was related to Muhammad, but it may also have been because of his religious character (some said that Ali had made his forehead shiny from praying so much).

The Muslims were now gaining control of many lands. Ali wanted to be closer to these lands so he made a new capital in what is now Iraq. By this time, there was fighting going on *between* Muslims. Ali's main Muslim enemy was Mu'awiyah. Ali tried to avoid war with Mu'awiyah, but not all Muslims thought Ali was right. One man wanted war with Mu'awiyah so much that he killed Ali with a poisoned sword.

The Umayyads take control

When Ali died, Mu'awiya seized control of all Muslim lands. He made himself caliph. Then he moved the Muslim capital to Damascus in Syria.

Mu'awiya was from the Umayya clan. The **Umayyad** family ruled the Muslims right up until 750.

Later, some Muslims accused the Umayyad caliphs of behaving more like kings than caliphs, but perhaps this is not fair. After all, the Umayyads had to adapt to new challenges. Islam was expanding rapidly. The caliphs now had many lands to rule.

STEP 1

On pages 21 and 22, find one example of:
- a disagreement over *who* should lead;
- a new idea about *how* to lead;
- a reason why it was difficult for Muslims to stay united.

Think

- Once the Muslims ruled many lands, why might their style of ruling have to change?

Ali's family fights on

The disagreements about who should lead, and how, did not stop...
After Ali was killed, his supporters became more and more worried
by the new Umayyad dynasty and its leader Mu'awiya.

One of Ali's sons wrote to Mu'awiya:

> You, Mu'awiya, take authority you do not
> deserve. You have no merit in religion... Give
> up your stubborn lies. You know that I am
> more entitled to be caliph than you in the
> eyes of God and all worthy people.

Mu'awiya wrote back:

> If I believed that you could protect the
> community better than I, and that you were
> stronger in protecting Muslims, I would do as
> you ask. But I am more experienced and older
> than you.

Letters quoted by a Shi'ite historian, al-Isfahani (897-967).

Supporters of Ali decided something had to be done about
the Umayyads (especially when Mu'awiya made his own
son caliph!). In 680, they encouraged Ali's son, al-Husayn,
to challenge the Umayyads. This famous story explains
what happened next:

Think

● What qualities did
Mu'awiya say that a
caliph needed?

Al-Husayn set out with about 200 followers. At a place called Karbala, by the river
Euphrates, al-Husayn met several thousand troops sent by the Umayyad Caliph. Al-
Husayn refused to surrender. His followers dug a trench and filled it with fire. But the
Umayyad army cut off their water supply. Parched with thirst, al-Husayn's troops
fought on. But there was no hope.

After the battle, the Umayyad general cut off al-Husayn's head, took it to Damascus
and gave it to the Caliph.

Ali's supporters became known
as Shi'at Ali (the party of Ali).
They were later called **Shi'ites**.

Today, the anniversary of
al-Husayn's death is a day
of mourning for Shi'ite
Muslims. Karbala, in Iraq,
is their holy city.

*Modern Shi'ite Muslims
act out what happened
at Karbala*

The Umayyads are destroyed (except one!*)

There were other reasons why some Muslims were unhappy with how the Umayyads ruled. The Umayyads treated foreigners as if they were inferior to Arabs. This made people in the old Sasanian empire angry. Their ancient civilisation was older than the Arabs'! Besides, Muhammad had said that all Muslims were equal. Why should they be treated differently? From 743 more and more Muslims rebelled against the Umayyads. The main rebel leaders were the **Abbasids**. They were descended from Muhammad's uncle 'Abu al-Abbas.

The Abbasids wrote poems attacking the Umayyads' ability to rule. They also used verses in the Quran to show that wicked, unfair government was very wrong. The Abbasids said that the Umayyads were not true caliphs.

These writings leave historians with lots of questions. Because so much was written against them, it is hard to judge whether the Umayyads were good or bad leaders! What we *do* know is that in 747 the Abbasids rebelled. Dressed in black clothes, they carried black banners.

Within three years, the Abbasids were successful. By 750, they had killed all the Umayyads (except one…!*).

STEP 2

On pages 23 and 24 find one example of:

- a disagreement over **who** should lead;
- a difference of opinion on **how** to lead;
- a reason why not all Muslims were united.

Thinking your enquiry through

History teachers are always asking you questions. It's time **you** asked the questions…

There won't always be answers! But finding the right question is a good place to start. This is what historians do. Historians are ready to ask hard questions. Then they use evidence and join debates with other historians in order to find the best answer that they can.

Make a 'Little Book of Questions' to help an historian. First, list the Muslims' difficulties. (That bit is easy – just use what you found for your Steps.) Then do the thinking bit: write some questions that you think historians should be asking about the Muslims' difficulties. Try starting your questions like this:

- How do we know…?
- Are there any sources about…?
- Why did some Muslims decide to…?
- What did Muslims think about…?
- Was …… really so bad?
- How effective was…?

* Just one Umayyad escaped. He fled far away. Look out for him in Enquiry 6.

So far, so fast

4

Why did Islam spread?

Despite all the early struggles, something extraordinary was happening. Islam was becoming a world religion. At the same time, the Muslims were establishing the largest **empire** the world had known. In the first century after Muhammad's death, Muslim armies burst out of the deserts of Arabia:

- They marched north and east into the **Sasanian Empire**, conquering the lands that are now Iraq and Iran.

- They marched north and west into the **Byzantine Empire**, conquering Syria and Egypt.

- They marched so far east that by 705 they had conquered Afghanistan. By 711 they had reached Sind in northern India and Samarkand in central Asia.

- They marched west into Africa. By 700, they controlled the whole of the north African coast.

- In 711 they invaded Spain. Only in France, at the battle of Poitiers in 732, did they finally stop.

But I don't get it. The early Muslims faced such difficulties!

And how could it have spread so **far**?

Yes, how could Islam have spread so **fast**?

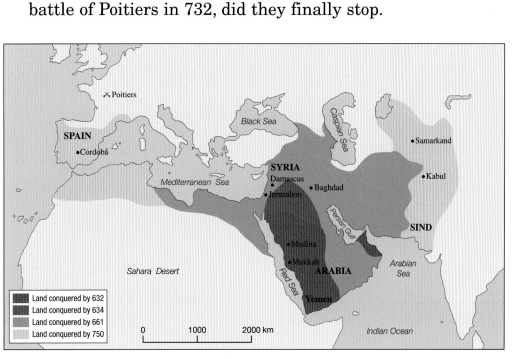

The expansion of Islam from the time of Muhammad until 750

The expansion of Islam map showing:
Poitiers, Black Sea, Caspian Sea, SPAIN, Cordobá, Samarkand, SYRIA, Damascus, Mediterranean Sea, Jerusalem, Baghdad, Kabul, Persian Gulf, SIND, Medina, Makkah, ARABIA, Arabian Sea, Sahara Desert, Red Sea, Yemen, Indian Ocean

Land conquered by 632
Land conquered by 634
Land conquered by 661
Land conquered by 750

0   1000   2000 km

Your enquiry

You are going to find causes of the spread of Islam. Using these causes, you will be able to create your own **historical explanation**. At the end of the enquiry you will make a diagram to help you explain why the power of Islam spread so far.

STEP 1

Read the first six 'Cause Ideas' on pages 26 and 27. Sum each one up into something short and simple. For example, you could shorten Cause Idea 2 into this:

Old empires taken by surprise!

This will be your cause card. Keep your cause cards carefully. You will use them in your diagram.

CAUSE IDEA 2

The Sasanians and the Byzantines never expected trouble to come from Arabia. The Arab tribes seemed too busy fighting each other! What danger could they possibly be to the great Sasanian and Byzantine empires? These great empires were content to control the border tribes and to enjoy trade with the caravans. They had never tried to conquer Arabia. Its land and people were too poor to be any use. Besides, these empires were too involved in their own war to notice the new power of Islam.

Nothing prepared them for the great victories of the Arab armies. So when large Arab Muslim armies attacked them, the Sasanian and Byzantine empires were taken completely by **surprise.**

CAUSE IDEA 1

During Muhammad's life, the Sasanian and Byzantine empires were at war with each other. When this war was over, these empires were not ready for another one. Neither side had any strength left.

CAUSE IDEA 3

Muslims believed that God wanted them to bring Islam to many more people. They believed that God was on their side. This strong faith gave them courage in battle.

CAUSE IDEA 4

Christians and Jews were not forced to convert to Islam. They just had to pay a special tax to their new Muslim rulers. The tax was lower than the one they had paid to the Byzantines.

This letter was sent by a famous Muslim general nicknamed 'the sword of Islam'. He sent it to the leaders of the lands he was about to invade. It gives us another clue about why the special tax may not have been unwelcome.

> In the name of God, the Merciful and the Compassionate.
> Become Muslim and be saved. If not, accept protection from us and pay the tax. If not, I shall come against you with men who love death as you love to drink wine.

Letter from Khalid ibn al-Walid, written in 633; quoted by Muhammad ibn Jarir al-Tabari, writing in the early tenth century.

CAUSE IDEA 6

Peoples in Egypt and Syria had another reason to hate their old rulers. This was to do with religion. Christians in Egypt and Syria were a different kind of Christian from their Byzantine rulers. The Byzantines tried to stamp out all kinds of Christianity other than their own. They also persecuted Jews.

Amazingly, some Jews and Christians found their new Muslim rulers more tolerant of their religions than their old rulers had been! Muslim rulers often protected Christians and Jews. Muhammad had said, "He who wrongs a Jew or a Christian will have me as his accuser on the Day of Judgement".

Some Jewish and Christian communities actually even grew:

Example 1: Some Jewish communities in Palestine became stronger once the Byzantines had gone. Many Jews returned to Jerusalem in the seventh and eighth centuries.
Example 2: Some Christians in Iraq found they were left in peace once the Sasanian rulers had gone. They were even able to build more monasteries and churches.

CAUSE IDEA 5

Many people living in Byzantine or Sasanian lands hated their rulers. The Byzantine and Sasanian rulers demanded high taxes to pay for their expensive wars. The Byzantines and Sasanians were hated so much that sometimes the Muslim Arab armies were welcomed as **liberators**.

One ninth-century Muslim historian tells us that Christians and Jews in the city of Hims in Syria begged the Arab soldiers to stay. When the Byzantines were finally defeated, they welcomed the Muslims back from battle with loud music and dancing.

Think

Remind yourself what religion the Byzantines were (try page 4). How does this make Cause Idea 5 seem rather surprising?

Now make more cause cards using Cause Ideas 7 to 14. (You will have to think hard to find the tricky cause in Cause Idea 13, but talk about it and you might succeed.)

CAUSE IDEA 7

The Arab tribes saw wealth in the lands they invaded. Fighting Muslim wars was a chance to get rich with war booty. One Arab general said to his soldiers before a battle in Iraq in 635:

> This land is your inheritance and the promise of your Lord. God allowed you to take possession of it three years ago. You have been tasting it and eating from it, and you have been collecting taxes from its people and taking them into captivity...
> You are Arab chiefs and important men, the chosen of every tribe, and pride of those behind you. If you aim for the world hereafter, God will give you both this world and the hereafter.

Adapted from an account by a Muslim historian, Muhammad ibn Jarir al-Tabari, in the early tenth century.

Think

What do you think this Arab general meant by 'tasting' the land and 'eating from it'?

CAUSE IDEA 8

The Arabs were skilful at all kinds of fighting. They had an amazing cavalry that could move very fast. The Sasanians and Byzantines were slow-moving in their heavy armour. With their light armour, the Arabs could use speed and surprise. They could travel long distances with few supplies. Living in the desert made them tough.

Illustration from an eleventh-century Greek chronicle showing Byzantine soldiers fleeing from an Arab army.

Think

What differences can you see between the Arab and Byzantine soldiers?

CAUSE IDEA 9

The Muslim forces had amazing weapons like ballistae (which the Greeks and Romans had used). Ballistae were giant slings used to throw enormous stones which could smash through the walls of cities.

CAUSE IDEA 10

As the Muslim forces moved into North Africa, they had to fight the **Berber** peoples who lived there. Some Berbers became dedicated Muslims. This made the Muslim forces even stronger. The Berbers helped the Arabs to conquer much of Spain by 720.

CAUSE IDEA 11

The Arabs built up their power at sea. This helped them to conquer the northern parts of Africa by around 700.

CAUSE IDEA 12

In the past, the Arab tribes had fought each other. Now, for the first time, they were united by Islam. Once the Arabs were united, they were powerful.

CAUSE IDEA 13
(WATCH OUT! THIS CAUSE IDEA IS TRICKY!)

Think

Cause Idea 13 may not *seem* like a cause of Muslim success at all. But read it and think... How do you think this might have helped Islam to spread?

Although the Muslim armies had speedy success, the Muslim faith sometimes spread more slowly. For about 100 years after bursting out of Arabia, Muslims made up only about a quarter of the people in all the lands they ruled. Many Jews, Christians and people of other religious faiths carried on being just that... Jews, Christians and people of other faiths!

Many Jews and Christians did later convert to Islam, but that process took time. Islam often spread slowly by people converting other people, not by rulers forcing their new subjects. When studying the early centuries of Islam, historians have found examples of Jews, Muslims and Christians borrowing books, stories and ideas from each other.

CAUSE IDEA 14

Things were certainly not always peaceful between Muslims and non-Muslims. Sometimes violence continued after the conquests. Where there were revolts and rebellions the Arab armies were strong enough to crush them.

Using pages 30 and 31, find two more cause ideas of your own. Turn your ideas into two cause cards.

By 750, the main Arab conquests were over. But the spread of Islam did not stop. The armies were followed by Arab merchants and traders. These Muslim traders now helped to spread Islam.

African peoples had a rich trade in gold and ivory, salt and slaves. Ancient trade routes linked the Mediterranean with the grasslands and forests south of the Sahara desert. Arab and Berber traders soon got involved in this trade. As they travelled to the African kingdoms across the Sahara, they took their Muslim faith with them. In 1010, the ruler of Gao in western Africa became Muslim. In 1087, a Muslim university was founded nearby at Timbuctu. By 1100, most people on the southern edge of the Sahara had become Muslims.

Arab merchants also sailed the Indian Ocean. They set up trading settlements on the coasts of eastern Africa, India, Indonesia and China. They sold luxury goods from Arabia, such as decorative metalwork, painted pottery and carpets.

The Great Mosque at Djenné in western Africa was built in the fourteenth century. Its mud-brick walls have been replaced many times, but the first mosque would have looked something like this.

The extent of the Muslim world by 1500

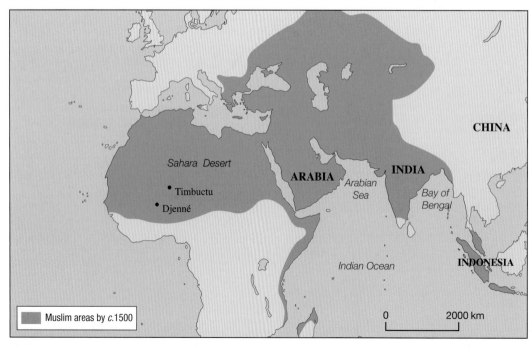

CHINA

Sahara Desert

ARABIA

INDIA

Timbuctu

Arabian Sea

Bay of Bengal

Djenné

INDONESIA

Indian Ocean

Muslim areas by *c.*1500

0   2000 km

Muslim teachers and missionaries soon followed the traders. They had great success in Africa and Asia. The people of central Asia were nomads who lived by herding cattle and fighting. These people were called **Turks**. Later, Turkish armies carried Islam deep into India, although traders and missionaries also played a part. Missionaries and traders from India then took Islam to Indonesia and the Philippines, where many people converted from the thirteenth century onwards.

Muslim trade created remarkable links across Europe, Asia and Africa. You might be surprised to learn where these Arab coins were found...

... in a tenth-century Viking grave in Sweden!

Thinking your enquiry through

You now have about 16 cause cards. You are going to use these cards to experiment with different ways of **explaining** the spread of Islam.

In pairs or threes, try out these different diagrams:

IMPORTANCE
Arrange your cards in a long line showing which ones you think were *most important*.

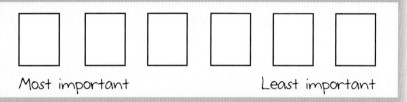

LINKS
Arrange your cards to show how one cause (or group of causes) is linked to another.

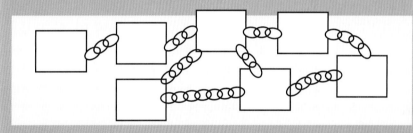

TYPES
Sort your cards according to *types*. See if they fall into particular groups. Decide what each group should be called.

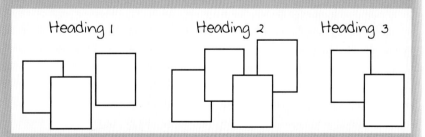

Now it is time to *talk* about why Islam spread, using your diagrams. Because you made different diagrams, your class will be able to hear different kinds of explanation. You can then discuss which kind of diagram gives the *best* historical explanation for why Islam spread.

"All the treasures of the world"

What was so special about Baghdad?

This photograph of Baghdad, Iraq's capital city, was taken in 2003. When we look at it, it is hard to believe that Baghdad was once one of the richest and most beautiful cities in the world. During the twentieth and twenty-first centuries, the people of Baghdad have experienced much suffering. In April 2003, American and British troops invaded Baghdad and ended the rule of Iraq's dictator, Saddam Hussein. In the years that followed, Baghdad became a difficult and dangerous city. Bombed buildings were in ruins, clean water and electricity were in short supply and fighting continued. A thousand years ago, Baghdad was a very different city.

By the middle of the eighth century, **Islam** had spread from Arabia to as far as Spain in the west and India in the east. It could take up to two years to travel from one end of the Islamic world to the other. At first, this vast **empire** was ruled by the **Umayyad** dynasty from their capital in Damascus. However, in 750, the Umayyads were defeated by a rival dynasty called the **Abbasids**, who moved the capital to Iraq. In 762, the Abbasid **caliph**, al-Mansur, decided to build a new capital on the site of a small village: Baghdad.

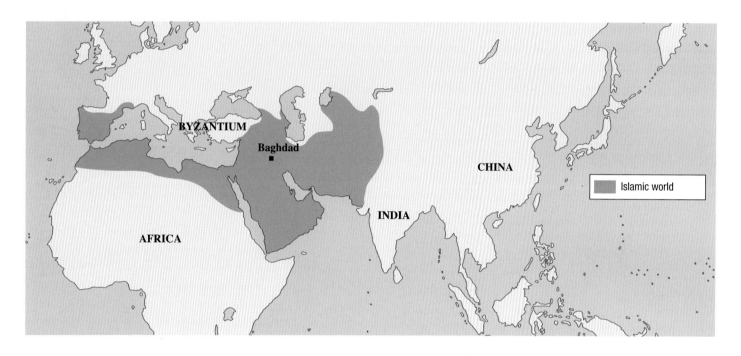

Think

● Look at the map and explain how Baghdad was in a good position to connect to Africa, Byzantium, India and China.

Al-Mansur chose the perfect place for his new city. Baghdad was built between two rivers – the Euphrates and the Tigris – within a web of connecting canals. The two great rivers flowed through a flat, wide plain of black, fertile soil. This rich agricultural land meant that the people of Baghdad could be easily supplied with wheat, barley, rice, dates and other foods. Baghdad's position also meant that the city was connected to the whole of the Islamic world and to the distant lands of Africa, **Byzantium**, India and China.

Map showing Baghdad, the Islamic world and beyond in 750

Your enquiry

During the eighth and ninth centuries, the Abbasid caliphs built the beautiful city of Baghdad. They also brought goods and ideas to Baghdad from all over the world. A ninth-century historian wrote that Baghdad contained "all the treasures of the world". In this enquiry, you will make a Baghdad treasure box to contain treasure cards that describe the special features of Baghdad. At the end of the enquiry, you will use your treasure box to explain what was so special about Baghdad.

The Caliph's Round City

The Abbasid caliph, al-Mansur, paid out huge sums of money to build Baghdad. He decided on a striking design for the city: his huge, new capital would be perfectly round. The walls and buildings of Baghdad would be made from large sun-dried bricks. Al-Mansur paid good wages to attract tens of thousands of workers to build Baghdad. Today, nothing remains of al-Mansur's Round City, but early descriptions of al-Mansur's massive building project give us some idea of what the city looked like.

2 We think that the space between the caliph's palace and the walls was used by the caliph's soldiers and officials.

1 At the centre of the Round City was the Grand **Mosque**. This was a square building with a large central courtyard. Here al-Mansur would preach to the congregation at Friday prayers.

9 Next to the Grand Mosque was the Caliph's palace. The huge green dome at the top of the palace could be seen by travellers as they approached the city. At the centre of the palace was the audience hall, where the caliph met important visitors.

8 A network of canals surrounded the Round City. These supplied water to farms and allowed food and other goods to be brought into the city by boat. The people of the city often travelled by boat too.

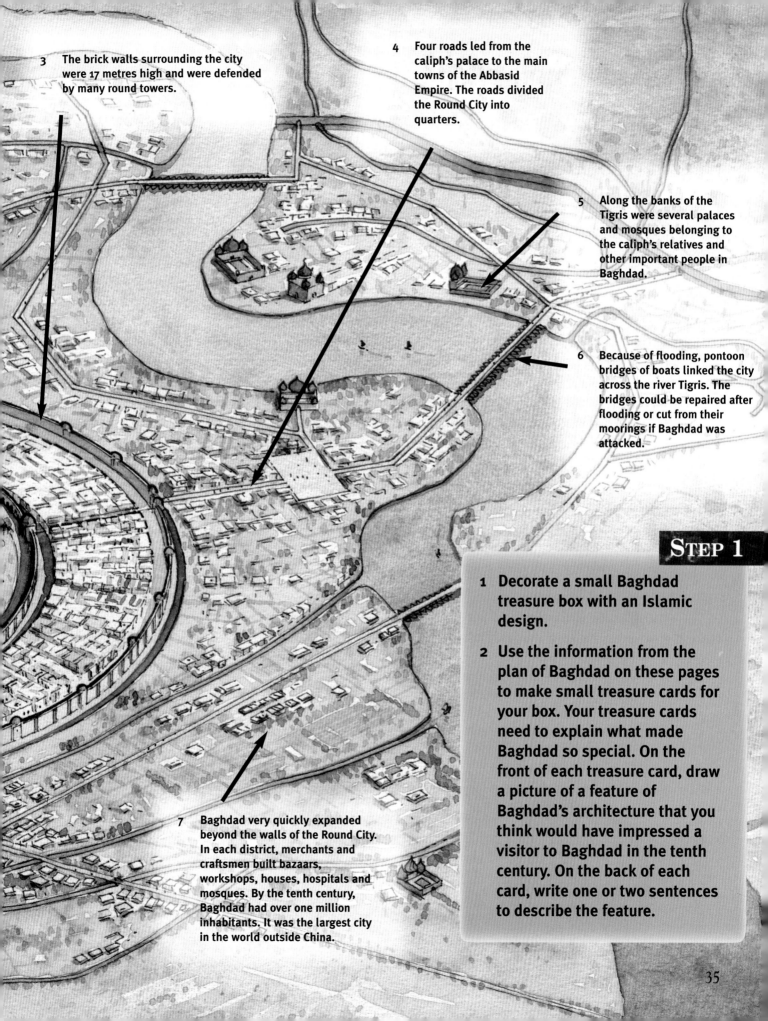

3 The brick walls surrounding the city were 17 metres high and were defended by many round towers.

4 Four roads led from the caliph's palace to the main towns of the Abbasid Empire. The roads divided the Round City into quarters.

5 Along the banks of the Tigris were several palaces and mosques belonging to the caliph's relatives and other important people in Baghdad.

6 Because of flooding, pontoon bridges of boats linked the city across the river Tigris. The bridges could be repaired after flooding or cut from their moorings if Baghdad was attacked.

7 Baghdad very quickly expanded beyond the walls of the Round City. In each district, merchants and craftsmen built bazaars, workshops, houses, hospitals and mosques. By the tenth century, Baghdad had over one million inhabitants. It was the largest city in the world outside China.

STEP 1

1 Decorate a small Baghdad treasure box with an Islamic design.

2 Use the information from the plan of Baghdad on these pages to make small treasure cards for your box. Your treasure cards need to explain what made Baghdad so special. On the front of each treasure card, draw a picture of a feature of Baghdad's architecture that you think would have impressed a visitor to Baghdad in the tenth century. On the back of each card, write one or two sentences to describe the feature.

A city of scholars and books

The House of Wisdom

The Abbasid caliphs created one of the most beautiful cities in the world, but they wanted Baghdad to be more than just a beautiful city. They wanted to make their capital into a city of learning and of new ideas. Traders from Baghdad brought goods, knowledge and ideas from different parts of the world. The caliphs also sent scholars to search for new knowledge in **Persia**, Byzantium, northern Africa, India and China. These scholars collected treasured texts and brought them back to Baghdad. During the ninth century, Baghdad became a city of scholars and books.

The centre of learning in ninth-century Baghdad was the House of Wisdom. The caliph brought scholars to the House of Wisdom from all over the Islamic world. He paid the scholars well, whatever their religion. The scholars translated Greek, Persian, Indian and other early texts into Arabic. But these curious and open-minded men did more than translate. The scholars of the House of Wisdom often added their own comments to the ancient texts. Much of the knowledge that was collected, copied and commented on in Baghdad eventually reached Europe through Islamic Spain and Sicily. It still affects many aspects of our lives today.

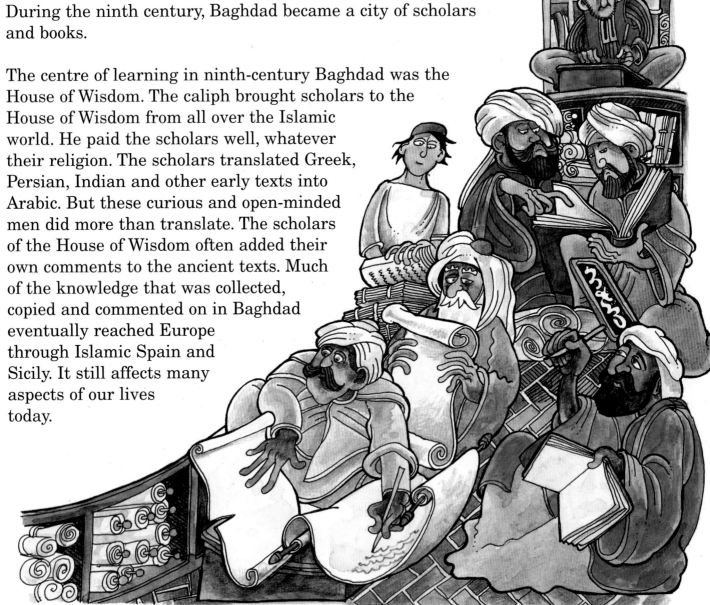

Paper, books, libraries and madrasas

Think

- How have you used paper since you got up this morning? (Yes, you can include wiping your bottom!)

It is easy to take paper for granted, but our lives would be very different without it. Baghdad traders brought back knowledge of paper-making and wood-block printing from China in the eighth century. Paper mills were built along the banks of the river Tigris and Baghdad was soon well-supplied with this new product. Paper made it possible to produce lots of copies of the same book at a low cost.

Baghdad soon became a city of bookshops and libraries. By the tenth century, the city had over a hundred booksellers. In the late tenth century, the catalogue of one bookseller, Ibn al-Nadim, listed thousands of books available in Baghdad at that time. Some people were able to build up huge private libraries. One scholar refused to take a job in another city because he said that it would take 400 camels to transport his books.

The most impressive libraries were in the city's religious colleges. These colleges, which appeared in the twelfth century, were known as **madrasas**. The caliphs or other wealthy individuals set up the madrasas and paid teachers good salaries to pass on their knowledge of important texts to their students. In the thirteenth century, when universities were first built in Europe, they followed the Islamic model.

A thirteenth-century picture showing a teacher and his students working in a well-stocked library

Think

- Find the books on the library shelves.

- In what ways do you think the madrasas made Baghdad a special city?

Muslim minds change the world

You might be wondering why the ideas of Islamic scholars in Baghdad were so important. Let's find out about five ways in which **Muslim** minds changed the world.

1. Mathematics

The scholars of Baghdad were fascinated by mathematics. They translated many of the ancient texts on geometry. Muslim engineers used this knowledge to build mosques, palaces, canals and bridges. Perhaps the greatest achievement of Muslim mathematicians was the development of the Indian system of numbering. It was so much simpler than Roman numerals. The Baghdad scholars based their system of numbering on the decimal place and the use of a small circle for zero. Without the idea of zero, we would not have computer software or the Internet.

2. Astronomy

The stars were very important to Muslims. For their prayers, Muslims had to know the direction of Makkah from wherever they happened to be. They also needed to know when each new moon would appear in order to work out their religious calendar. In the ninth century, some Baghdad astronomers built observatories on top of their houses and gazed at the night sky. The early ninth-century caliph, al-Mamun, helped the astronomers by paying for a large observatory at the House of Wisdom. Baghdad astronomers worked out the movements of the planets. They also developed the astrolabe, a small metal instrument that travellers could use to find their position using the stars.

3. Geography

The Abbasid caliphs were keen to find out about the lands they ruled and about the world beyond. The caliphs encouraged the geographers at the House of Wisdom to write books and to make maps. In the ninth century, one famous geographer, Ibn Sarayun, wrote a book that described all the seas, islands, lakes, mountains and rivers known to him. The maps and geography books produced in Baghdad were much more advanced than anything that Europeans produced at that time.

4. Science and technology

The scientists of Baghdad made many important discoveries. Muslim chemists worked out how to produce ink, paint, soap and glass on a large scale. Physicists developed the magnetic compass from an ancient Chinese idea. They also worked out that our eyes see by receiving rays of light that bounce off objects. The Muslim scholars of Baghdad developed the science of optics on which our modern contact lenses and cameras are based. Another piece of technology developed in Baghdad was the water-wheel. In the eighteenth century water-wheels would power the first industrial revolution in Europe.

5. Philosophy

Islamic scholars gave a lot of thought to the big questions of life. Al-Ghazali was the son of poor, illiterate parents, but, in the eleventh century, he became one of the most important philosophers, lawyers and teachers in Baghdad. One of the questions that al-Ghazali thought about deeply was the education of children. He wrote that children should not boast about their parents' wealth, and that they should be taught not to love money. Al-Ghazali described money as "a deadly poison".

Think

● What do you think about al-Ghazali's ideas?

STEP 2

It's time to make another set of treasure cards for your Baghdad treasure box. Use the information on pages 36–39 to select people, places, inventions and ideas that you think helped to make Baghdad such a special place for learning and knowledge. Design the front of each card. On the back of each card, write one or two sentences to describe the person, place, invention or idea.

Muslim medicine

This picture, made in the eighth century, shows Islamic doctors delivering a baby by Caesarean section. The ancient Greeks had developed this way of saving a baby if the mother died while in labour.

Caesarean births were just one medical development that the Muslims learned from their translations of ancient medical texts. The Abbasid caliphs collected a huge library of medical books. Scholars at the House of Wisdom translated them into Arabic. From the Greeks, the Muslims learned how to examine a patient carefully before prescribing a treatment. They started to use alcohol as an antiseptic and learned about the use of drugs and herbs to treat diseases.

Muslim scholars did not just copy the ancient Greeks. They also added medical knowledge from their own studies. One of the greatest scholars of medicine in tenth-century Baghdad was al-Razi, known in the West as Rhazes. Rhazes kept detailed

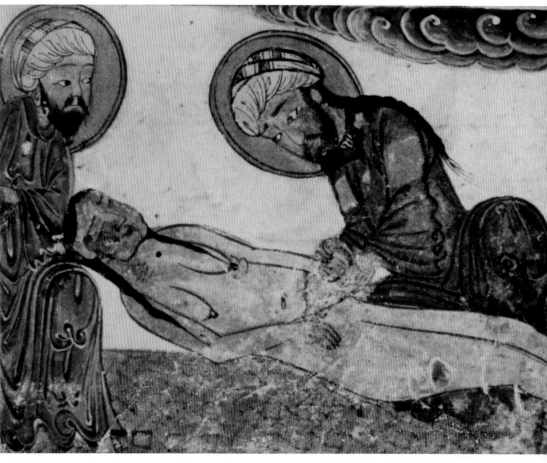

A fourteenth-century picture of a baby being born by Caesarean section

notes on all the patients he treated and wrote nearly two hundred books on medicine. These included books on kidney and bladder stones and on the treatment of smallpox and measles. Perhaps Rhazes's most important work was a huge encyclopaedia of medicine called *al-Hawi*.

For each disease listed in *al-Hawi* Rhazes gave the views of Greek, Indian, Arab and Persian writers. He then added notes from his own observations of patients and gave his own opinions about the disease. Rhazes was not afraid to rely on his own observations when they disagreed with the ideas of earlier doctors.

In this picture you can see a doctor at work in a hospital. Islam taught that sick people should be looked after and that hospitals should be built to care for them. The Abbasid caliphs built a number of hospitals in Baghdad. The hospital buildings were very spacious and were built around garden courtyards, as Islamic doctors believed that gardens and running water helped people to get better quickly. The hospitals in tenth-century Baghdad included a pharmacy, library and small mosque. Qualified doctors cared for the sick and helped to train medical students. This was much more advanced than anything in Europe at the time.

A fourteenth-century picture of a doctor examining a patient

STEP 3

Use the information on Muslim medicine to select aspects of medicine that you think helped to make Baghdad such a special city for the development of medical knowledge and practice. Now make your final set of treasure cards for your Baghdad treasure box.

Thinking your enquiry through

It's time to play "All the Treasures of the World"! Play with a partner, taking it in turns to pick a treasure card from each other's Baghdad treasure box. Your challenge is to explain what made the 'treasure' on your chosen card so special. You can score a maximum of six points for each card:

1 point – if you can explain what made this treasure so special to the people of tenth-century Baghdad.

2 points – if you can explain the origins of this treasure.

3 points – if you can explain how this treasure still affects our lives today.

It may not be possible to score six points for each card you choose. Keep your score as you play the game. The winner is the player with the highest score when all the cards have been used. Good luck!

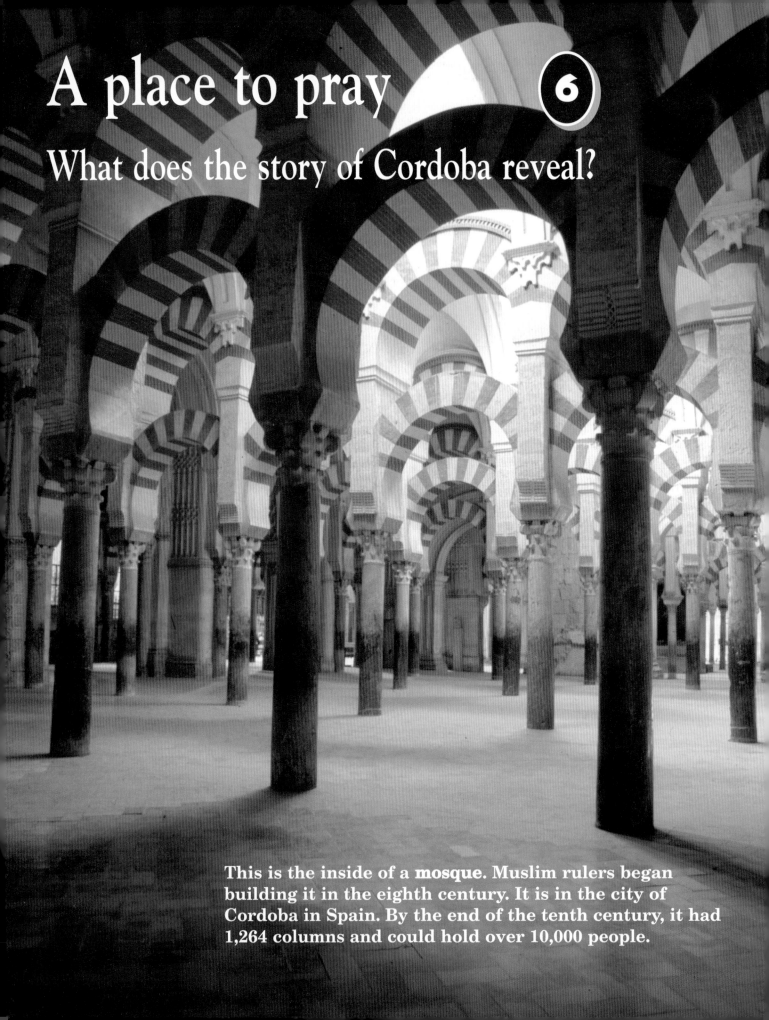

A place to pray
What does the story of Cordoba reveal?

6

This is the inside of a **mosque**. Muslim rulers began building it in the eighth century. It is in the city of Cordoba in Spain. By the end of the tenth century, it had 1,264 columns and could hold over 10,000 people.

By the tenth century, the city of Cordoba had over 214,000 houses and 80,000 shops. Her buildings were a beautiful mixture of Arab, north African and Roman architecture. Cordoba was bigger than Cairo and richer than Rome. Some said it was even more beautiful than Baghdad.

The part of Spain conquered by Muslims was called al-Andalus. The history of al-Andalus is made up of layers of peoples from different places, religions and cultures.

- The **Greeks** came to trade there.
- Then **Carthaginians** traded there.
- Then the **Romans** invaded.
- Then the **Visigoths** invaded.
- Then, in 715, came the **Muslims** (often called **Moors**). These were Arabs and African peoples.

Your enquiry

Cordoba is a special place for anyone studying history. The story of the mosque and the city around it **reveal** so much about the history of Islam. Cordoba's story also reveals how Muslims and non-Muslims lived together and treated each other.

You are going to think about what Cordoba's story **reveals** to historians. Working in groups of four historians, with post-it notes in four colours, each of you must search for one theme:

1: Muslims' love of **art** and **beauty**

2: **connections** between Cordoba and the wider Muslim world

3: **skills** or **knowledge** of Cordoba people

4: encounters between **Muslims, Christians** and **Jews**

A homesick ruler

Abd al-Rahman had much to be thankful for. He was now the **Emir** of al-Andalus. He was also fortunate to be alive! As the last of the **Umayyads**, in 750, he had fled from the new rulers of the Islamic world, the **Abbasids**. What a journey he had had! He had even swum for his life across the river Euphrates.

But Abd al-Rahman was homesick. Far away from the places of Syria that he loved, he would never see his homeland again. He planted a palm tree to remind him of home. He wrote a poem about it.

...Born in the West, far from the land of palms,
How like me you are, far away and in exile!
In long separation from family and friends
You have sprung from soil in which
you are a stranger,
And I, like you, am far away from
home.

But it was no use being homesick. Abd al-Rahman had to get on with ruling his new land. The first thing to do was to create a place for the Muslims of Cordoba to pray.

Hall of light

Close to the river, there was a Christian church, the church of St Vincent. In 751, Abd al-Rahman made an agreement with the Christian Visigoths. He bought part of the church for the Muslims to worship in. Some sources describe Abd al-Rahman as tall and fair-haired with one eye. Imagine him meeting the Christians to arrange the sale. We imagined it like this:

The church became a place where Muslims and Christians worshipped God, each in their own way. But the Muslim population grew. There was not enough space in just half a church for all of Cordoba's Muslims. Something had to be done.

Abd al-Rahman remembered the fine mosque in Damascus with its beautiful mosaics and its architecture inspired by the **Byzantine** Christians. Why couldn't Cordoba have something like that?

So in 784, Abd al-Rahman I bought the other half of the church and some land next to it. This would be the site of Cordoba's new mosque. Abd al-Rahman I let the Christians build churches in other parts of the town.

But there were still so many problems to be solved…

This space is wide – how shall we support the roof without lots of walls?

It mustn't feel gloomy. How can we keep a feeling of space and light, even in the middle?

How will we make our mosque beautiful? We don't have the skills or materials for the mosaics we had in Damascus.

What sort of stone shall we use?

The Muslim architects looked around them. They saw pillars and columns in Roman monuments and in Visigothic houses and churches. These fine pillars were decorated with geometric shapes and vine leaves. Why not collect these and use them?

This was their **first brilliant idea**.

But there was another problem. The pillars were too short. In Syria, they had been so much taller. The prayer hall needed to honour God. The Muslims wanted a high, light building, not a dark, dingy place.

Again the Muslim architects looked around them. They looked at the arches in the old Roman aqueducts all over Spain. How strong these were! They looked at the horseshoe-shaped arches in the Visigothic buildings. They put these two ideas together and so created **another brilliant idea:** a layer of semi-circular arches on top of the horseshoe-shaped arches! This created space and light, even in the middle of the wide hall.

Looking up, Muslim worshippers saw a ceiling of spaces, all woven together and going on forever. The arches hung above them like palm trees, the symbol of their distant homeland.

It was a wonderful system. Wherever you stood, everything could be seen at the same time. There were no walls, only delicate patterns of light. The pattern of red brick and white limestone was like space repeating itself. It was perfect symmetry, flowing together forever, like the never-ending love of God.

Abd al-Rahman was pleased. This was more than he had dreamed. Nothing had been seen like it in the world.

STEP 1

Take your post-it notes, historians. Cut out thin arrows. Stick these on your textbook wherever you think our story reveals something about your special theme.

45

City of learning

The mosque gets bigger

About 70 years later, another emir made big changes to the mosque. Abd al-Rahman II wanted the mosque to be even bigger and even more beautiful. He added eight new aisles. This took 15 years. Cordoba's mosque was now one of the most important religious places in the Muslim world.

Here is a plan of the changes to the mosque of Cordoba. Find the sections built by Abd al-Rahman I and II. You can see that there were plenty more changes to come!

AL MANSUR 978–1002

AL-HAKAN II 961–976

ABD AL-RAHMAN II 822–852

ABD AL-RAHMAN I 750–788

ABD AL-RAHMAN III 912–961

Wise men and wonders

It was a good time to love beautiful things. Al-Andalus was changing. Cordoba was becoming one of the most important centres of art and learning in the world. Cordoba was full of papermakers, glassmakers and silkworm breeders. The city was famous for its crafts of gold, ivory, jade and leather.

Abd al-Rahman II liked to bring things to Cordoba as well: jewellery from Arab countries, exotic animals from Africa and books from everywhere. He brought wise men and artists to his court. One of these was Ziryab – a gifted musician. Ziryab means 'blackbird', (a nickname that came from his beautiful voice). Ziryab added a fifth string to the lute. He taught the Caliph's court to play chess and he was famous for his cooking.

Abd al-Rahman II built colleges where people could learn about science and industry. He also improved agriculture. Landowners and farmers all over Spain copied his irrigation schemes. Rice, sugar cane, orange and grapefruit trees had all been introduced by the Muslims. By the ninth century, they were exporting olives, grapes and figs.

Arabs, Mozarabs and anti-Arabs

During this time, there were attacks by Christians on Muslim lands and some Muslim expeditions against Christian lands. But Abd al-Rahman II still worked hard to be on friendly terms with non-Muslim lands. He even received special representatives from the Christian emperors of Byzantium.

Arab ways of speaking and dressing, writing and learning were spreading fast, even to Christians and Jews. Many Christians in al-Andalus loved Arabic poetry, especially the moving love poetry that travellers carried between Cordoba and Baghdad. There were many religious books in Latin, but nothing like the many beautiful poems, songs and stories that the Arabs had.

Even Christian religious books and services were soon translated into Arabic. A Christian who loved Arabic language and culture became known as a Mozarab, a sort of 'wanna-be Arab'.

But some Christians in Cordoba were worried by how popular Arabic writings were becoming. They feared the beautiful, new Arab stories would replace the old Latin books of the Christian Church. One Cordoban Christian complained crossly:

Christians love to read poems and romances of the Arabs; they study the Arab theologians and philosophers. Who now reads the Latin writings on the Holy Scriptures? Alas, young Christians read and study Arab books with enthusiasm. They gather big, expensive libraries and they despise Christian literature as unworthy.

One group of Christians tried to stop the spread of Arab ways and Muslim beliefs. A Christian called Eulogius encouraged his followers to say the Muslim faith was wrong. He encouraged them to become **martyrs** by provoking Muslims to violence. This led some Muslims to attack Christian churches. Eventually the Muslim authorities executed the followers of Eulogius.

Other Christians liked Arab culture and were content with Muslim rule. Abd al-Rahman II did not force Christians to convert to Islam. He accepted Jews and Christians, and let them worship freely. Many Muslims thought Christians, Jews and Muslims had something very important in common: they were all 'Peoples of the Book'.

Think

● What do you think 'Peoples of the Book' meant?

Later in the ninth century, Cordoba suffered many troubles. There were droughts, locust plagues and terrible diseases. Some Moorish lands tried to break away from Cordoba's rule.

STEP 2

Hunt for examples of your special theme on pages 46 to 47. Now place your 'posts-its'.

A city of art

A caliph for Cordoba

It took Abd al-Rahman III 20 years to regain the Moorish lands that had broken away. After that, he showed the Muslim world that Cordoba was important. He made himself **Caliph** (to challenge the caliphs of Baghdad) and 'Representative of Allah on Earth' (to challenge the rulers of Egypt).

Many non-Muslims helped in Abd al-Rahman III's government. He chose a Jew as chief doctor. He even gave important roles to a Christian bishop.

Abd al-Rahman III changed the way Cordoba looked. All over Cordoba, he built schools, libraries, public baths and hospitals (with special, new sections for the mentally ill). Poets and philosophers thrived in Cordoba, too. It was a place for new ideas, great works of literature and beautiful art.

Abd al-Rahman III also improved the mosque. He made the courtyard bigger and he built a **minaret**, 48 metres high. Some say the minaret was topped by three golden spheres. Christian architects later copied it in church towers and spires.

Most beautiful mosque in the world

When Abd al-Rahman III died in 961, his son, Al-Hakan II, looked around him at the still-growing city. The very next day he made a decision. He would extend the mosque yet again. Soon the prayer hall was 104 metres long.

But Al-Hakan II wanted more. He wanted a mosque fit for a ruler of the Muslim world. Using the finest designers and craftsmen, he filled the mosque with some of the most beautiful art ever seen. He even asked the Byzantine emperor for advice on mosaics for his **mihrab**.

Al-Hakan II's mihrab. A mihrab shows the direction to face when praying. Al-Hakan II made his into a small room made of marble.

In front of the mihrab, al-Hakan II built a maqsurah. It is a kind of screen, making a special room where the caliph could pray. Look at its light, delicate arches. The Cordobans copied these arches from their rivals in Baghdad. The shapes made from flowers, plants and the natural world also came from Baghdad but the Cordobans found their own way of making these beautiful.

City of three religions

Al-Hakan II loved learning. He encouraged new books, especially on medicine and science. Tenth-century writers speak of a library of over 400,000 books. People were now writing, borrowing, exchanging and reading books so quickly that the copyists could hardly keep up! Al-Hakan II speeded things up by building a copying and bookbinding workshop. The workshop also produced Christian books in Greek, Latin and Arabic.

Al-Hakan II tolerated other religions. Jews had settled in Spain in the third century, but the Christian Visigoths had persecuted them. When the Muslims came, they made **alliances** with the Jews. Jews lived in their own part of Cordoba, (as they did in most medieval cities), but many held important jobs. By the time of al-Hakan II, there were Jewish doctors, writers, officals and businessmen.

Think

● Why did people call al-Hakan II 'Lord of the three religions?

STEP

Hunt for examples of your special theme on pages 48 to 50. Now place your 'post-its'.

Dangerous times

The mosque's last extension

When al-Hakan II died, his son was only 11, so a senior official ruled for him. This ambitious man was famous for raids into Christian kingdoms. In 981, when he returned from one of these raids, he was named al-Mansur bi-llah ('Victorious in the name of Allah'). Al-Mansur was less tolerant than earlier rulers. He ordered books not containing correct Muslim ideas to be destroyed. At the same time, al-Mansur kept the lands of the Caliph united and strong. With so many attacks by Christians from the north, these were dangerous times.

Al-Mansur also extended the mosque. It now grew to 24,000 square metres – the biggest mosque in the world. The builders had to knock down houses to make space. One old lady refused to leave her house until al-Mansur had built an identical one complete with its orange tree and patio! Archaeologists have found the remains of both houses.

This was the last extension. Cordoba's mosque was complete.

Death and destruction in the city of light

During the early eleventh century, weak or greedy rulers fought each other to take control of Cordoba. This part of Spain became known as the Kingdom of the Gangs. Yet this was no time for weakness. The Christian kingdoms of the north were trying to conquer Muslim lands.

Then, in 1013, Cordoba was attacked from another direction. The **Berbers** of north Africa broke through the city walls and massacred 20,000 people. A poet, Ibn Hazam, wrote about how those born in the 'city of light of the west' watched the death of friends and loved ones.

After this…

Where has my power gone?

The caliphs lost all their authority.

The population of Cordoba shrunk.

The size and wealth of the city fell.

Meanwhile, the Christians were becoming stronger. The Cordobans strengthened their city walls, but this was not enough. In 1090, the Muslim rulers in Spain begged for help from a northern African Muslim tribe called the Almoravids. The Almoravids, and the Almohads who came after them, were a different sort of Muslim from the Arab Muslims who first came to Cordoba. They were not tolerant of different ideas, let alone different religions!

But the 'city of light' did not die easily. In the twelfth century, there was one last marvellous time when knowledge, ideas and thinking grew. Here are two famous names from this period.

One was a Muslim.

Ibn Rushd, also known as Averroes, wrote books on medicine, mathematics, astronomy and philosophy. His work is important in all religions to this day.

One was a Jew.

Maimonedes was a clever Jewish doctor who explained all the teaching of Judaism in one huge book before he was 33! Maimonedes linked science and religion. He also linked morals and medicine. He said that if we are to be good and know God, we should have healthy bodies. He also said that Jews should care for people of all religions and get involved in the real world.

But with the Almohads in charge, even these thinkers were not safe. Soon, non-Almohad Muslims had to give up their land. Many Jews fled to Christian kingdoms. Maimonedes fled to another Muslim land, Egypt. There he was welcomed. He even became the personal doctor to the **Sultan**!

Christian Cordoba

During the twelfth century, Christian forces kept trying to take Cordoba, but they did not succeed. Then, in December 1235, on a moonless, stormy night, the Christian king led a huge attack. It turned into a long siege. On 29 June 1236, Cordoba surrendered. In July, Muslims were expelled from the city.

A few hundred Muslims were allowed to return to the city after 1236. The Christians wanted the skills of Muslim artists so that they could decorate the new Christian churches. These Muslims could only worship in a small mosque in a separate part of Cordoba. They had to wear special marks on their clothes.

The great mosque of Cordoba was no longer a place of Muslim worship. Part of the mosque was turned into a small Christian chapel.

But for about two hundred years, no big changes were made to the mosque. It still looked more or less as it always had...

until the sixteenth century...

At the beginning of the sixteenth century, the Archbishop of Cordoba decided he did not want to go on making small changes to the mosque. He wanted to build a big cathedral, right in the middle of it.

The citizens of Cordoba were not pleased. They knew that the mosque of Cordoba was a special building. The Archbishop's plans would destroy it.

Think

● Why do you think that **Christians** in the city wanted to keep the mosque as it was?

The town council decided not to build the cathedral. They also announced that any bricklayers, stonemasons and craftsmen who started work on it would be killed.

The town council and the Archbishop quarrelled so much that they went to the Emperor, Charles. This powerful man ruled much of Europe and all of Spain. Charles supported the Archbishop. He gave his permission and the cathedral was built. An enormous Christian building was built inside a Muslim one. In this photograph of the cathedral, you can just see the Muslim arches on either side.

The rest of the mosque is still standing all around it. But the cathedral:

- destroyed the wide spaces stretching on like the endlessness of God;
- broke the flowing patterns of light;
- made no link with the art around it.

Eventually, Charles saw it for himself. Even he was horrified:

"If I had known this, I would not have let you touch the old building. You have built what you might have built anywhere. You have destroyed what was unique in the world"

Our story is finished. Find examples of your special theme. Place your final 'post-its'.

Thinking your enquiry through

So what *did* the story of Cordoba **reveal?** Rejoin your group. Show your fellow historians where you put your arrows.

You now need a large piece of paper. You are going to draw or paint your own celebration of Cordoba's history. You must fill the paper with pictures of events, places or people from this enquiry.

Then cut about eight little shutters in the paper. Make sure they open and close. (It will look a bit like an advent calendar!). Now stick another piece of paper behind. Open each shutter and, underneath, write the title of one (or more!) of your four themes. Don't just write any old theme! Your group must decide *which* theme (or themes) that bit of your picture **reveals.**

Threats from beyond **7**

How can we know what Muslims thought of Crusaders and invaders?

Look at this fine old map. It was made in 1154 by al-Idrisi, an Arab **Muslim** geographer.

Do you recognise the parts of the world shown in the map? It shows most of Europe, northern Africa and a large part of Asia. Can you see the British Isles, Spain and Italy?

Are you still puzzled? It will help if you know that twelfth-century Arab map-makers used to put north at the bottom of their maps. The map makes more sense to our eyes when we turn it upside down!

Your enquiry

If we don't know how to use sources like the medieval Muslim map, we can make some very silly mistakes. In this enquiry, you will advise a rather hopeless historian on how to use sources properly – and you will make something special to help him with his work.

You will be studying the war-filled years between 1000 and 1300 when the Islamic world came under attack from outsiders. With your help, the hopeless historian should learn all sorts of fascinating things about the beliefs, hopes and fears of medieval Muslims and what they felt about these threats from beyond.

Saracens and Franks

All through history, people have been puzzled and alarmed by others who are different from them. At the start of the Middle Ages, Christians in northern Europe knew little about Muslims and their advanced civilisation. They called them '**Saracens**' and wrongly believed that they were all dark, long-haired tent-dwellers who wandered desert lands, following strange religious beliefs.

As for medieval Muslims, they knew quite a lot about Christians who lived along the Mediterranean Sea, but they knew far less about those who lived in northern Europe. In about 950, a Muslim called al-Masudi wrote this description of northern Europeans, or '**Franks**' as Muslims called them:

The Franks lack a warm sense of humour; their bodies are large, their character is coarse, their customs rude, their minds dull and their tongues heavy. Their skin colour is of such an extreme white that they appear blue. Their skin is thin and their flesh rough. Their eyes are blue. Their hair is smooth and reddish due to the damp fog. Their religious beliefs are unreliable, which can be traced to the type of coldness and lack of warmth. The further north they reside, the dumber, more vile and primitive they are.

Think

- Name three countries in northern Europe where you think these 'Franks' lived.

- Do you think al-Masudi admires these Franks? Give reasons for your answer.

I'm not going to use this source. The writer is **biased**!

Well done for spotting the bias… but don't throw the source away!

Biased sources can be really helpful. It all depends what we are trying to find out! For example…

Our rather hopeless historian wants to throw away al-Masudi's source because he can see that it is **biased**. Luckily, someone is there to help him.

1 Give three examples from the source to show that al-Masudi is biased against the Franks.

2 Give some reasons **why** al-Masudi's description might be biased against the Franks.

3 Copy the second historian's final words of advice and add some examples to show how the bias in al-Masudi's description can help historians to understand the thoughts and feelings of medieval Muslims.

Holy Land – but whose land?

For Jews, Christians and Muslims, the area shown in yellow on the map is very special. It is called the Holy Land. At its heart is Jerusalem, the city where the great Jewish temple once stood, where Jesus Christ died and where Muslims believe the prophet Muhammad was taken up to heaven to meet God. Over the years, many different groups controlled the Holy Land and Jerusalem.

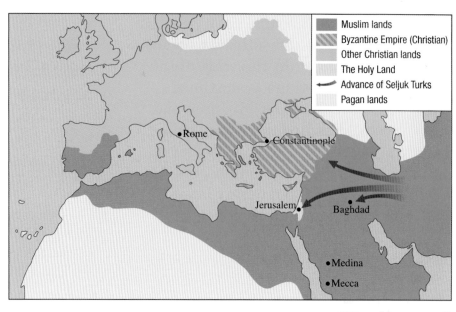

Muslim and Christian lands c. 1070

From **395, Greek Christians** ruled it as part of the **Byzantine Empire**. Most of its people were Christians, although many were Jews.

Then, in **638, Arab Muslims** took the Holy Land. Most inhabitants were still Christians or Jews, but many became Muslims over time. The Christians and Jews paid a special tax to their Muslim rulers who allowed them to carry on living and worshipping there.

Around **1077, Turkish Muslims** called **Seljuks** took control of the Holy Land. They had moved west from central Asia, setting off struggles between different Muslim groups and making it hard for Christian pilgrims from Europe to visit Jerusalem. When Seljuk armies invaded his lands, the Byzantine Emperor called for help from western Christians and their leader, the Pope.

Then, in **1099, European Christians** (Franks) invaded the Holy Land and captured Jerusalem. The Pope had promised them rewards in heaven for joining this **crusade** (holy war) to restore Christian control of Jerusalem. These Franks from France, Germany and Italy were the first Christians to control Jerusalem for over 450 years.

Think

- Why do you think the Franks captured Jerusalem?

- What would you expect the Muslims to do when the Franks arrived?

"How can you slumber?"

The Christian attack on Jerusalem was a bloody affair. When the Muslims refused to surrender, the Crusaders followed the custom of the time and showed no mercy. One Crusader described how he and other Franks "waded through blood up to our ankles".

Muslims living near Jerusalem expected their **Abbasid** rulers to send help –

but nothing happened. One Syrian Muslim called al-Harawi travelled over 950 kilometres to see the **Caliph** at Baghdad. With his head shaven as a sign of mourning, he bravely challenged the Caliph and his court with these words, captured by an Iraqi poet of the time:

Think

● Do you think al-Harawi is more upset by the violence of the Crusaders or the failure of the Caliph to send help?

How can you slumber in the shade of comfort and safety where life is as soft as orchard flowers? How can your eyes sleep while your Muslim brothers in Syria have no dwelling place, other than the saddles of camels and the bellies of vultures? Must the foreigners feed on our shame! Beautiful young girls have been shamed and now hide their sweet faces in their hands! White swords' points are red with blood, and the iron of brown lances is stained with gore! This is war, and the infidel's sword is naked in his hand, ready to be sheathed in men's necks and skulls. For fear of death, the Muslims are evading the fire of battle.

The Caliph was moved. Tears flowed. A group of advisers investigated what could be done **but still nothing happened**. Since the Seljuk Turks had arrived, the Caliph had no real power. The Muslim world had lost its unity and the arrival of the Franks in distant Jerusalem was not a serious concern in Baghdad. The grateful Franks occupied large parts of the Holy Land.

STEP 2

Oh dear! Our hopeless historian thinks the Iraqi poet's account of al-Harawi's speech is "too poetic" to tell us anything useful.

Write a simplified version of al-Harawi's words that captures his main points in a clear and direct way.

The rule of the Franks

This picture is taken from a Christian manuscript written around 1170. It shows one of the Crusaders, Baldwin I, taking control of the settlement of Edessa. In the years just before and after the fall of Jerusalem, similar scenes took place in Crusader settlements in and around the Holy Land. For most of the period between 1100 and 1291, it was Christians, not Muslims, who ruled these lands.

In their desire to keep control or to increase their power and wealth, the rulers went to war from time to time. These wars were not always about religion: sometimes Christian and Muslim lords would help each other against common enemies. Meanwhile, ordinary Christians, Muslims and Jews continued to live as neighbours.

Think

- In the picture, find:
  a) Baldwin
  b) Christian subjects
  c) Baldwin's knights
  d) Muslim subjects.

- Why do you think the artist has shown Muslims in the background?

One man's view

An educated Muslim called Usamah ibn Munqidh became a trusted friend of Christian knights in the Crusader kingdoms. In 1175, he wrote about the Franks and "their curious mentality". Despite his genuine friendships, Usamah never really saw the Franks as his equals. He may not directly say this, but he **implies** it throughout his book, as the extracts on the next page show.

A Muslim and a Christian playing music together, from a thirteenth-century music book

Extract 1 – The meal and the marketplace

Franks who have mixed with Muslims over many years are much better than the ones who have recently arrived. But they are the exception. For example, I went to the home of a Frankish knight who served me with extraordinarily clean and delicious food. Later, as I was in the marketplace, a Frankish woman grabbed my clothes and began to mutter words in their language.

I was immediately surrounded by a large crowd of Franks. I was convinced that death was at hand. Then, that same knight approached. He said to the woman, "What is the matter?" She replied, "This Muslim has killed my brother". The knight shouted at her, saying, "This is a merchant who neither fights nor attends a fight." He also yelled at the crowd and they all dispersed.

Extract 2 – The offer... and the refusal

A Frankish knight who had become my close friend said to me: "My brother, I am leaving for my homeland and I want you to send with me your 14-year-old son. He will come to our country where he can learn wisdom and **chivalry**. When he returns, he will be a wise man". These words would never come out of the head of a sensible man. For even if my son were to be taken captive in war, it could not bring him a worse misfortune than carrying him into the lands of the Franks.

(Usamah politely declined the offer!)

Extract 3 – The monks and the Sufis

I entered a church. Inside were 10 old monks, their bare heads as white as combed cotton. They wore crosses on their chests. They offered hospitality to all who needed it. The sight of their piety touched my heart, but it also saddened me for I had never seen such devotion amongst the Muslims. But later, nearby, I saw about a hundred prayer mats, and on each one was a **Sufi** Muslim, his face expressing serenity and devotion. I thanked Almighty God that there were among the Muslims men of even more devotion than those Christian priests.

STEP 3

Our hopeless historian does not know what we mean by the word "implies". Help him by copying this chart and adding more examples from the extracts. (We have done one for you.)

How Usamah praises the Franks	How Usamah implies that Muslims are better than the Franks
"The Franks who have mixed with Muslims over many years are much better..."	He suggests that Muslims have a good influence on Franks and pass on their high standards.

The merciful

At first, Muslim rulers lacked the unity that they needed to remove the Franks. But by 1176, a powerful new leader had united large parts of Syria, Palestine and Egypt. His name was Saladin (Salah al-Din).

Saladin was ashamed that Muslims were ruled by Christians. He called for a **Jihad**. Jihad can refer to the Muslim's struggle to be holy and to live a good life, but it can also mean a holy war against the enemies of Islam, especially those who have invaded Muslim lands.

Painting of Saladin, c.1180

In 1187, he crushed a Christian army in battle at Hattin and went on to recapture Jerusalem. Saladin could be a ruthless soldier; he once personally executed a brutal Crusader knight. But his fairness and generosity at other times won him the title 'Saladin the Merciful'. When Jerusalem surrendered, he lived up to this name and allowed the Christians to leave in safety, as was the custom in wars at that time.

Once the Christians had gone, Saladin made his triumphant entry to Jerusalem and led the rejoicing of the crowds. After a week spent clearing away all Christian symbols from the **mosque**, a great service of thanksgiving was held. The mood of the occasion is clear from the words of the preacher, Ibn al-Zaki:

> Glory to God who has bestowed this victory upon Islam and who has returned this city to the fold after a century of perdition! Honour to this army, which He has chosen to complete the re-conquest! And may salvation be upon you, Salah al-Din Yusuf, you who have restored the lost dignity of this nation!

Think

- What impression do you get of Saladin from his portrait above?

- According to Ibn al-Zaki, what was so special about the recapture of Jerusalem?

60

The merciless

The Franks fought back after losing Jerusalem in 1187. They led many new Crusades, but they never again had as much power in the Holy Land. However, the Muslim world was far from safe.

In the East another, a **far greater threat** was looming. It came from the **Mongols**, the armies of Genghis Khan, who called himself 'World Conqueror'. They had swept across most of Asia, into China and through Russia into eastern Europe.

The Muslim historian, Ibn al-Athir, captured the feelings of his fellow Muslims soon after the merciless new invaders first attacked Muslim lands in 1218:

> The events I am about to describe are so horrible that for years I refused to speak of them. It is not easy to announce the death-blow of Islam. O, would that my mother had not born me or that I had died and become a forgotten thing before this happened! History does not contain anything like it. Nay, it is unlikely that mankind will see the like of this calamity until the world comes to an end.
>
> This catastrophe passed over the lands like clouds driven by the wind. For these were a people that had emerged from the confines of China, taking possession, destroying, slaying and plundering. They slew all who withstood them.
>
> We ask God to grant victory to Islam and the Muslims, for there is none other to aid, help or defend the True Faith. But if God intends evil to any people, naught can avert it, nor have they any ruler, save Him.

Gengis Khan died in 1227 and the Mongols withdrew… for a while. Then, in 1258, a new Mongol leader, Hulegu, launched an even more overwhelming attack on Iraq. He destroyed Baghdad and murdered the last Abbasid caliph. Some accounts say the Mongols killed 800,000 Muslims. They certainly devastated the canals and water systems that had made the region so fertile. It never fully recovered.

If Islam was to survive, it needed a new Saladin. But while Saladin had been merciful, the new hero was almost as merciless as the Mongols.

Think

- How does al-Athir make it clear that the Mongols were a serious threat to Islam?

- Al-Athir died in 1233. Do you think he believed Islam was safe by then?

Victory

It seemed that nothing could stop the Mongols. But in September 1260, at the battle of 'Ayn Jalut near Nazareth, they were defeated for the first time ever.

The Muslim army that beat the Mongols was led by the **Mamluks**. These Turkish soldier-slaves had been bought to serve the Sultan of Egypt, but in 1250 they assassinated him and took his place.

The Mamluks' greatest general was Baybars. He was enormously tall and dark, and was blind in one eye that had a large white spot on the eyeball. Soon after the battle Baybars knifed his own leader and made himself the new sultan of Egypt.

Although the Mongols were **pagans**, some Franks had planned to join forces with them against Islam. This made Baybars determined to destroy the Crusader settlements as he established his own mighty Mamluk empire.

One of his greatest victories came in 1268 when he seized a city called Antioch. Baybars boasted of his conquest by sending a letter to the Christian prince who had once ruled the city. The letter almost certainly exaggerates what Baybars actually did at Antioch, but it helps us to sense how he felt about his victory.

God who gave you Antioch has taken it away again. If you had been there, you would have seen your knights prostrate beneath horses' hooves, your houses stormed by pillagers and ransacked by looters, your women sold for a coin of your own money! You would have seen the crosses in your churches smashed, the pages of your false Testaments scattered, and tombs overturned. You would have seen fire running through your palaces, your dead burned in this world before going down to the fires of the next. Then you would have said: "Would that I were dust, and that no letter had ever brought me such tidings!" Your soul would have left your body for sadness.

In 1291, the Mamluks finally expelled the last of the Franks. Within a few years it was clear that the threats from Crusaders and Mongols had disappeared. The Muslim victory was complete.

Thinking your enquiry through

The time has come for our hopeless historian to sum up what he has learned. You now have to help him with a really valuable skill: choosing and using good quotations from sources.

1 Copy the chart below. On the left, you can read what the historian wants to say. He has done well this time. It's a good summary, but it needs to be supported by evidence from sources. From each section in this enquiry, choose ONE short quotation from a source that he could use to back up his statement. Choose words that capture the Muslim reaction really clearly. Write the quotation in the second column. In your final column, write the name of the author of the source, who he was and the date when the source was written.

Events and Muslim reactions	Quotation to support this view	Author and date
Around 950, Muslims knew little about the Franks but thought they were very different and rather strange.		
When Christian Crusaders captured Jerusalem in 1099, Muslims in the Holy Land were surprised that their leaders did not try to drive them out.		
Between 1100 and 1291, there were Crusader settlements in the Holy Land, and some Franks and Muslims developed greater respect for each other.		
Although the Franks caused problems, the Mongol invasions in the thirteenth century were a far more serious threat to the whole of Islam.		
Muslims were delighted with their victories that completely defeated the Franks by 1300.		

2 And finally... our hopeless historian won't always have you there to help him! So, design and make something to remind him how to use historical sources properly. It could be a bookmark, a paperweight or a screensaver, and it should include suitable images (e.g. old documents or artefacts). Above all, it must show at least one important piece of advice about using sources to make sense of the past.

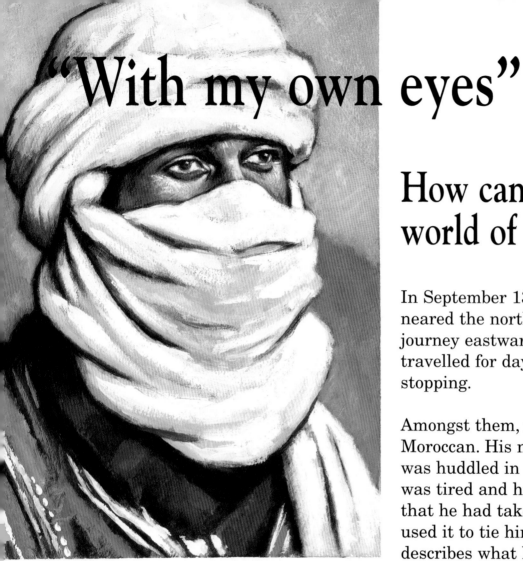

"With my own eyes" ⑧

How can we picture the world of Ibn Battuta?

In September 1325, a band of travellers neared the north African city of Tunis. Their journey eastwards had been hard. They had travelled for days and nights without stopping.

Amongst them, riding a donkey, was a young Moroccan. His name was Ibn Battuta. He was huddled in a long cloak of fine wool and was tired and hungry. He had such a fever that he had taken off his turban and had used it to tie himself into his saddle. He describes what happened next:

> The townsfolk came out to welcome us. On all sides they came forward with greetings and questions, but not a soul said a word to me, since there was none of them that I knew. I felt so sad at heart on account of my loneliness that I could not restrain the tears that started to my eyes. I wept bitterly.

An extract from the Rihla of Ibn Battuta, published c. 1355

Think

- In your imagination, picture the scene as Ibn Battuta arrived at Tunis.

- Compare your ideas with a partner. How were the pictures you imagined similar or different?

It is hard to believe, but this tearful, homesick young man became one of the greatest travellers the world has ever known. Over the next thirty years Ibn Battuta journeyed over 112,000 kilometres by foot, donkey, camel, cart and ship. He visited the far edges of the **Muslim** world and beyond. He went to west, north and east Africa, to Arabia, Russia, India and China. (See the map on page 72).

Before he died, his memories of these journeys were recorded in a book known as the Rihla or 'travels'. Those words are all we have to help us imagine the sights he must have seen.

Your enquiry

You are a picture researcher for a publishing company.

You have just received this email from your editor. She is setting you quite a challenge.

Read the email carefully as it tells you what you will be doing in this enquiry.

At the end of the enquiry, you will have to work with several others. You must prepare for a meeting with one of the editor's assistants who is coming to gather your advice and to ask you some tricky questions!

From: The editor

To: The picture research team

Subject: Advice please

As you know, we are publishing a modern version of the Rihla (journeys) of Ibn Battuta. We want it to be a really good interpretation of the world he knew.

The trouble is that the original Rihla had no pictures. It is full of fine descriptions and amazing tales about life all over the world in the fourteenth century. Ibn Battuta keeps saying "I saw these things with my own eyes" – and we want to help our readers by adding some pictures that give a good idea of what he actually saw.

This is where we need your help. We have summarised for you some of the things that Ibn Battuta saw. We have also included some pictures that we may want to use. We want you to tell us which ones we should use and why.

As you know, Islam has sometimes discouraged people from painting realistic scenes. It has been hard to gather a good selection of images. If we have included any that aren't really suitable, be sure to tell us. Good luck!

STEP 1

No one knows exactly what Ibn Battuta looked like. There are no pictures of him from his own lifetime (1304-c.1369). In his book he mentions that he had a beard and that he wore a large turban. He came from north west Africa where most people were dark-eyed and olive-skinned. But many others were quite fair with blue eyes, while some had dark black skin and hair.

One book includes this image of an Arab traveller. It was made in Baghdad in 1237. Your editor wants to use it to illustrate the story of his entry to Tunis (see page 64). Write a note to tell her whether you think she should do this. Explain your ideas and make helpful suggestions.

5

Mother of cities

In April 1326 Ibn Battuta reached Cairo in Egypt. It made quite an impression on him.

A modern photograph of Cairo showing the great Mamluk mosque of Sultan Hassan (on the left, completed c. 1363) alongside the Rifai mosque, (completed in 1900)

I travelled up the majestic Nile until I arrived at Cairo, mother of cities, boundless in multitude of buildings, peerless in beauty and splendour, the meeting place of comer and goer, the stopping place of the feeble and strong. She surges as the waves of the sea with her throngs of folk and can scarce contain them.

Extract from the Rihla of Ibn Battuta, published c. 1355

Cairo was the capital city of the **Mamluks**. These powerful slave-soldiers had defeated the Christian Crusaders and the **Mongols** and had created their own mighty empire. It stretched from Egypt to Syria.

Cairo could claim to be the heart of the Islamic world in the fourteenth century. It had over 500,000 inhabitants (about fifteen times the size of London at that time). The Mamluks filled the city with beautiful stone palaces and **mosques** set amongst its sprawling alleys.

As Ibn Battuta pressed his way through the people, donkeys and camels on its densely crowded streets, he would have seen markets filled with butchers, goldsmiths, leatherworkers, candlemakers and countless other trades.

An engraving of travellers overlooking the city of Cairo and the River Nile. Made in northern Europe c. 1600

Arabian illustration, 1237

And there were the **caravansaries**: Ibn Battuta would see thousands of these large inns as he crossed the world.

They were open courtyards surrounded by storage rooms on the ground floor overlooked by upstairs rooms where merchants and travellers would stay overnight. The largest had space for as many as 4,000 guests – and all their camels!

Arabian illustration, 1237

STEP 2

1. **Your editor wants to know which ONE of the pictures on page 66 she should use to illustrate what Ibn Battuta says about Cairo. Explain your choice carefully.**

2. **Your editor is keen to use a picture to illustrate what a caravansary was like in Ibn Battuta's time – or as close to his time as possible. Should she use either of the pictures on this page? Explain your answer.**

Makkah – the goal of our hopes

At this stage Ibn Battuta had no intention of travelling the world: he simply wanted to reach the holy Muslim city of Makkah.

In September 1326 he joined thousands of other Muslim pilgrims at Damascus. Groups as large as 20,000 travelled together for community and safety. Some were rich and travelled in joy and comfort but others struggled to survive the 1,600 kilometre journey in fierce heat by day and bitter cold by night. For the last 320 kilometres the pilgrims had to wear white robes to show their equality before God.

A late thirteenth-century illustration that most text books agree shows joyful pilgrims setting out for Makkah

A photograph of modern pilgrims circling the Kaaba at Makkah

In October 1326, Ibn Battuta and his fellow pilgrims finally reached the holy city, or as he called it "the goal of our hopes".

That very day, Ibn Battuta kissed the holy stone, circled the **Kaaba**, clung to its curtains, drank the holy water and prayed devoutly. He had faithfully completed the **Hajj**!

The great sea

By now Ibn Battuta had a taste for travel. From Makkah he journeyed north into Iraq and Iran before turning south again. In late 1328 he was at the port of Aden, on the coast of what he called "the great sea". From there, dhows (sailing ships) carried goods up and down the African coast and across the Arabian Sea to India.

Over the next two years Ibn Battuta sailed as far south on the African coast as Kilwa. This was the southern limit of the Muslim world. Islam had not spread far inland, but the coast was full of Muslim ports where merchants had grown rich.

Kilwa's wealth came from trade in gold from inland Africa. The **Sultan** of Kilwa was a powerful African who showed Ibn Battuta the great stone palace he was building on the highest point of his island. Ibn Battuta described him as "a man of great humility, who sits with poor brethren and eats with them".

A dhow from a thirteenth-century book. The crew appears to be Indian but the passengers are Arabs

Goods traded along the Arabian and east African coasts in Ibn Battuta's time:

Spices	Perfumes
Herbs for medicines	Plants for dyeing
Brass and bronze pots	Rice
Pearls	**Cowrie shells**
Porcelain	Ivory
Arabian racehorses	Gold
Pottery	Slaves
Animal skins	Books
Silk and cotton	

STEP 3

1. The editor wants to use the thirteenth-century picture of Muslim pilgrims on page 68 – but unfortunately another recent textbook says that it shows soldiers going into battle. Look closely at the picture and advise your editor whether or not she should use it.

2. Should the editor also include the photo of modern pilgrims? Explain your answer.

3. Your editor has decided to use small pictures to decorate the pages about trade at sea. Suggest SIX goods from the list provided that you think would look really interesting and show the variety of goods involved. Give reasons for your choices.

'The Shadow of God'

A Muslim ruler in India, from a sixteenth century painting

On his travels, Ibn Battuta heard of the Sultan of Delhi, known as the 'Shadow of God'. This powerful Muslim ruler was offering riches to educated foreigners who could help him govern his vast lands in India. Ibn Battuta was keen to help!

In 1331 he set off for India, travelling north through the area we now know as Turkey and east across the great open grasslands known as the Steppe. This was the home of the Mongols, who had once threatened to destroy Islam but were now Muslims themselves.

In 1333, Ibn Battuta made his way through Afghanistan and into northern India. Large parts of India had been ruled by Muslims since 1193, even though most of its millions of villagers were Hindus. Many of these people were desperately poor. Ibn Battuta even saw them eating animal skins to stay alive.

Life was different for the 'Shadow of God'. When he entered Delhi, elephants, richly decorated with silks and gems and fitted with small catapults, launched gold and silver coins into the crowds! Elephants featured in the Sultan's darker side as well: for no good reason he could turn against anyone. One of his favourite methods of execution was to have the victim tossed to and fro by elephants with swords tied to their tusks.

Despite these dangers, Ibn Battuta served the Sultan as a judge and administrator in north India for six years. He did once upset the Sultan, who arrested him. Ibn Battuta feared that he would be executed and prayed and fasted and recited the **Quran** for five days and nights. The next day he was set free, and the Sultan never mentioned the incident again!

Infidels ... and tears

In August 1341 the Sultan sent Ibn Battuta to China as his ambassador. After four years of curious misadventures, he reached Samudra in modern Indonesia. The prince of this small port made it the world's most easterly Muslim state when he converted to Islam in 1297. Things have changed: Indonesia is now the most populated Muslim nation on earth.

From Samudra, Ibn Battuta sailed north east and by 1346 he was in China. His year there was his only extended stay in a non-Muslim nation. The state did not use Arabic language or Muslim law. The cities were huge and customs seemed strange. Perhaps he was suffering from what we now call 'culture shock'. He felt far from home. In his book, he later explained:

The Chinese are **infidels**. They worship idols. The king is a Mongol descended from Genghis Khan. They eat the meat of pigs and dogs. In every city of China is a quarter where the Muslims live separately. When I saw Muslims it was as if I had met my family. One day I met a Muslim from very near my home town. He wept – and I wept too.

An eleven-headed god in a twelfth-century Chinese painting

When Ibn Battuta tried to explain Islam to leading Chinese scholars they would not treat his beliefs seriously. They refused to accept that there was just one God. No wonder that Ibn Battuta said "China was beautiful, but it did not please me". In 1346 he decided to head home to Tangier, far away in northern Africa.

STEP 4

1. There are no suitable images of the Sultan known as the 'Shadow of God'. Decide whether the editor should use the picture on page 70 instead. Give your reasons.

2. The editor is puzzled that she has not found any images of poor Indians from the fourteenth century. Explain why you think so few exist.

3. The editor wants to include an image that captures an aspect of Chinese life that Ibn Battuta found strange. What sort of image would you look for and why?

The final journey

It was late 1349 when Ibn Battuta reached his home town of Tangier – and learned that the Black Death had killed his mother just a few months ago. His father had died years before.

Ibn Battuta found it hard to settle back in his home town. He crossed to Spain and went to Granada – the last Muslim foothold in Europe. Then in 1351 he set off across the Sahara desert on his final journey. He wanted to see Mali, whose control of the west African gold trade made it fabulously wealthy.

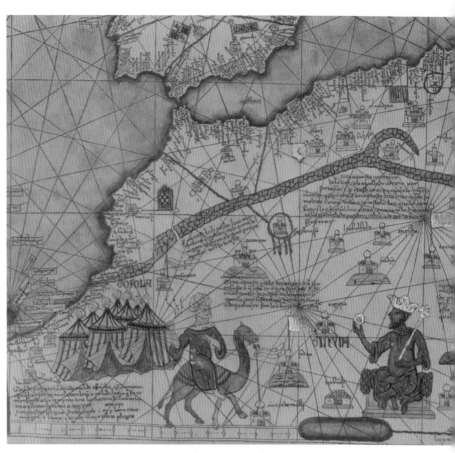

An Arab traveller meets a west African king. From a Spanish Atlas, 1375

Although Mali was a Muslim country, local tribal customs seem to have survived. Ibn Battuta was offended in many ways:

- officials refused to speak to him directly
- he was offered meals that he found unacceptable
- he saw servants grovelling in the dust before the ruler
- royal poets danced in animal masks and feather costumes
- female slaves stood in the court stark naked.

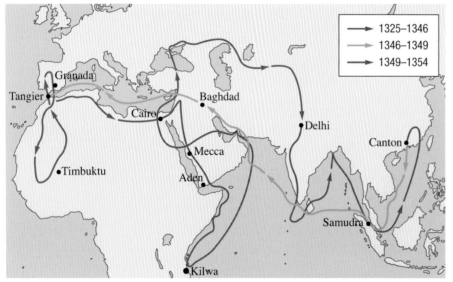

The travels of Ibn Battuta between 1325 and 1354 – a simplified map

After all his travels, Ibn Battuta never ceased to be amazed at how different life could be across the Muslim world.

The final destination

By 1354 Ibn Battuta had settled back in Morocco. We know little of his last years. It seems he died in 1368 or 1369 – but no one knows where.

Tourists are led to a tomb where his remains are supposed to lie, but there is no evidence to suggest that it is his real burial place. It seems odd that we know so much about his travels to the far corners of the world – but we do not know the final destination of this extraordinary Muslim traveller.

A photograph of what some claim to be the tomb of Ibn Battuta in Tangier

Think

- Why would anyone want to pretend that this is Ibn Battuta's tomb if it is not?

- If we cannot be sure that this is Ibn Battuta's real tomb, should its photograph appear in the book?

Thinking your enquiry through

1. Your editor thinks the picture on page 72 is so good that it should not only be used in the Africa section, it should also appear on the front cover of the book! She wants you to give her a balanced summary. List all the reasons FOR using it and then all the reasons for NOT using it.

2. Just in case she changes her mind, suggest one other image from all those you have seen that you think would make a good front cover. Give your reasons.

3. Your editor would like you to draft a fifty word catchy summary of what the book is about. It will appear on the back cover. It needs to capture the imagination of the reader and make them want to buy the book – but it must also give them an accurate understanding of who Ibn Battuta was, where and when he travelled and what he saw... with his own eyes!

4. Finally, your editor is sending someone (who may look surprisingly like your teacher) to gather your advice. Work in a group and share ideas to make sure you have really good answers to the questions raised in the Steps. He or she may 'hotseat' any one of you at any time. Your advice needs to be clear, confident, and well-supported with relevant detail.

The rose and its thorns

How did the Ottoman sultans show their power?

This is a portrait of the **Ottoman Sultan**, Mehmed II. In 1480, when the portrait was painted, Mehmed II had ruled the mighty Ottoman Empire for nearly 30 years. He was one of the most powerful rulers in the world.

You can see that the artist has shown Mehmed II sitting cross-legged, smelling a rose and holding a handkerchief. On his head, Mehmed wears the turban, a symbol of Ottoman power. Mehmed was a cultured man. He loved poetry, art and beautiful gardens. The Sultan was also very shrewd. Look how the artist has tried to show Mehmed deep in thought.

Mehmed II was also a great warrior who led his armies into many battles. That is why the artist has shown him with an archer's ring on his thumb. Some people think that the rose which Mehmed is holding represents the **Muslims** in his empire. His people are protected by Mehmed's powerful armies – the leaves and thorns of the rose.

Think

● Why do you think that Mehmed II would have been pleased with this portrait?

A portrait of Mehmed II, c.1480

The growth of the Ottoman Empire

This map shows where the Ottoman Empire had its origins in the early fourteenth century. It was here that Osman, the leader of a Turkish tribe, began to conquer his rivals in Anatolia (modern Turkey). Osman's successors went on to expand their territories into the **Byzantine** lands. You can see how far the Ottomans had spread by the beginning of Mehmed II's reign in 1451.

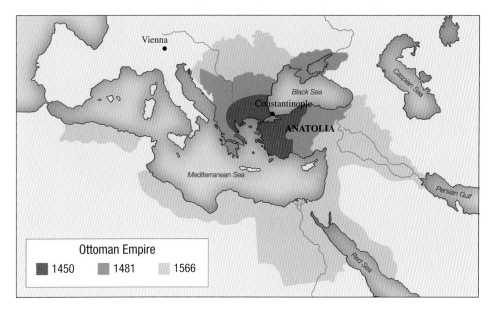

Map showing the growth of the Ottoman Empire

Think

● Use an atlas to find out which modern day countries formed part of the Ottoman Empire in 1566.

In 1453 Mehmed II captured the Byzantine city of Constantinople. He turned the city into the new capital of his empire. Mehmed II went on to conquer more territories. You can see, on the map, how much the Ottoman Empire had grown by the end of his reign, in 1481. No wonder he is known as Mehmed the Conqueror!

During the reign of Mehmed II's great grandson, Suleyman the Magnificent, the Ottoman Empire grew even more rapidly. By the time of his death, in 1566, Suleyman ruled over a huge territory which covered Turkey, north Africa, the Balkans, the Black Sea and parts of Arabia. The Ottoman sultans were at the height of their power.

Your enquiry

In this enquiry your challenge is to explain the different ways the Ottoman sultans showed their power. You will work as a researcher for a new three-part TV history series: "The Power of the Ottoman Sultans". A top presenter has been chosen for the series, but he doesn't know much history! You will need to provide the presenter with the big ideas for each programme. In order to capture the viewers' interest you will also need to suggest some scenes which can be brought to life using actors. The three programmes in the series will be: 1. The Sultan's army 2. The Sultan's palace 3. The Sultan's empire.

The Sultan's army

By 1452, all that was left of the Byzantine Empire was the city of Constantinople. On all sides, the city was surrounded by the Ottoman Empire. It was the beginning ofMehmed II's reign, and he was determined to increase his power by conquering Constantinople.

For many years, the Christian city of Constantinople had been in decline. But an attack on the city would not be easy. Earlier attempts to defeat Constantinople had all failed. The city was well protected by huge sea and land walls. All the way from the Golden Horn to the Sea of Marmara, snaked enormous walls, studded with strong towers. To prevent an attack by sea, the Byzantines had stretched a massive iron chain across the channel of the Golden Horn.

During the spring of 1453, Mehmed assembled 150,000 soldiers outside the walls of Constantinople. For months, the craftsmen of the Ottoman Empire had been making helmets, shields, javelins, swords and arrows. Mehmed had also paid for a deadly new weapon. In front of the Sultan's tents stood an eight-metre-long bronze cannon which fired stone balls weighing more than half a ton. Mehmed hoped that this monster weapon, and his other cannons, would blast through the city's walls.

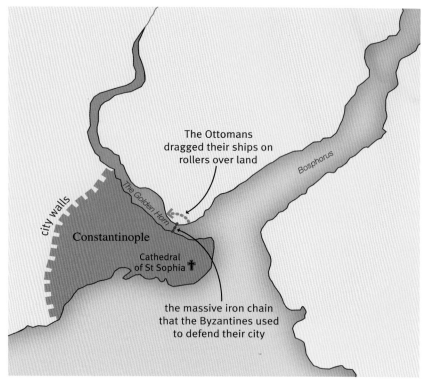

A map showing the siege of Constantinople, 1453

By 7 April, the Ottomans had surrounded Constantinople by sea and land. The attack began. After several days, the Ottoman cannons began to shatter the city's outer walls. But the Christians were able to patch the holes with bales of straw, wood and earth. The Ottoman army could not breach the walls. At sea, the Ottomans tried to break the iron chain protecting the Golden Horn. They failed. It was clear to Mehmed that the conquest of Constantinople would not be easy. He would have to tighten his grip on the city.

Mehmed thought of a very clever plan. Instead of trying to break through the chain across the Golden Horn he decided to carry his ships around it! His engineers and soldiers made a slipway of tree-trunks and planks which they greased with sheep's fat. They placed their ships on huge sledges and dragged them over the hill. Within a few hours, eighty ships had slithered, like killer crocodiles, into the waters of the Golden Horn.

Now Mehmed could begin his final attack on Constantinople. The Sultan ordered his war banner to be unfurled. In the early hours of 29 May, Ottoman troops, with their scimitars, cannons and siege towers, began a life or death fight for the city. After hours of fierce combat, they finally found a weak point in the city's walls. A small gate had not been properly secured, and the Ottomans pushed their way through. Ottoman soldiers flooded into the city and the defenders ran to protect their families.

Later that morning, Mehmed rode into the conquered city of Constantinople. Outside the Christian cathedral of St Sophia, he dismounted from his horse, scooped up a handful of dirt, and sprinkled it over his turban, in an act of humility. He entered the cathedral and began to think how he could convert it into a **mosque**.

A European painting of the siege of Constantinople, c. 1455

Think

● Why do you think Mehmed sprinkled dirt over his turban?

● In what ways did Mehmed show his power during the siege of Constantinople?

This European painting of Mehmed II's siege of Constantinople has put many of the key events together in one image.

Think

● Which parts of the story of the siege of Constantinople can you find in the painting?

In 1529, Mehmed's great-grandson, Suleyman the Magnificent, attacked another famous city – Vienna. Look carefully at the details of the attack in this picture.

Think

● Find:
the walls of Vienna and the defending soldiers
the Sultan's cannon
the red and yellow tents of the Ottoman leaders
the white silk wall which symbolised a fortress
the Sultan's war standard – six horse tails on
    a golden pole
the beautiful carpets spread out in front of the tents
the Ottoman leaders discussing the siege
the Ottoman soldiers with their
    scimitars, shields and spears

A painting of the Siege of Vienna

The sultan's army put up the biggest, best and most frightening camp-sites in history. At the end of a day's march a whole canvas city could suddenly appear in the fields. Even the Ottoman horses had their own canvas stables. When the sultan attacked Vienna again in 1683, the canvas city outside the capital was bigger than Vienna itself. It had neat rows of tented streets for the soldiers and gardens for the sultan and his officials.

The soldiers, who you can see at the bottom of the picture, were called Janissaries. These men were the sultan's most feared fighting force. From the plume at the top of his turban, to the tip of his tough red boots, the Janissary was a one-man fighting machine. He was also the sultan's loyal slave. When they needed more soldiers, the sultans forced Christian families in the Balkans to hand over their sons. The boys were taken to Constantinople, raised as Muslims, and trained to serve the sultan. Most of these boys became Janissaries. They were the sultan's loyal troops, and formed the highly-trained core of the Ottoman army.

STEP 1

It's time to plan your first programme for the new TV series, "The Power of the Ottoman Sultans". This programme should focus on how the Ottoman sultans showed their power through the army.

1 Make a list of three main ideas that you think the programme should include. For each idea explain why you think it should form an important part of the programme.

2 Imagine two scenes which could be brought to life using actors. For each scene write a paragraph describing the setting and action.

The Sultan's palace

Mehmed II rebuilt the ruined city of Constantinople as the new capital of his empire. Over the next twenty five years he brought people from all over the Ottoman Empire to make Constantinople the most important and beautiful city in the world. Mehmed encouraged Jewish and Christian craftsmen, as well as Muslims, to settle in the city.

At the point where Constantinople stretched out to the sea, Mehmed built his new palace – the Topkapi. The Sultan chose an isolated and wooded area, away from the noise and bustle of the city. The Sultan's new palace was more than a building: it was the heart of the Ottoman Empire from which all power flowed.

Think

● Find the Topkapi Palace.

● How many mosques can you find?

A sixteenth-century map of Constantinople

A plan of the Topkapi Palace

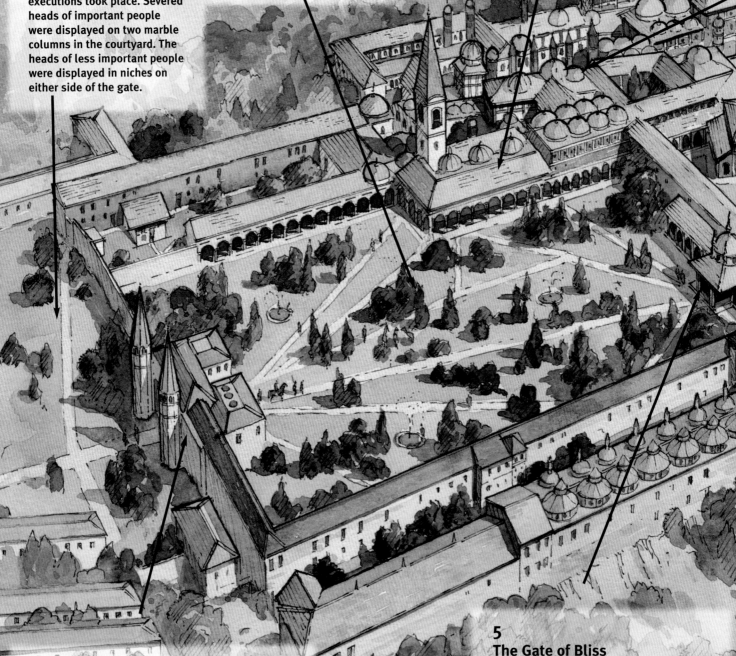

1

The First Court

This was the size of four football pitches. There were stables for the 4,000 horses, barracks for the guards, a hospital and workshops for the 600 craftsmen who worked in the place. Anybody could enter this part of the palace, but visitors were expected to be quiet. This was the place where executions took place. Severed heads of important people were displayed on two marble columns in the courtyard. The heads of less important people were displayed in niches on either side of the gate.

3

The Second Court

This huge space was filled with lawns, cobbled paths, fountains and cypress trees. Gazelle grazed here for the pleasure of the sultan. The courtyard was surrounded by a shaded arcade. Doors led from the arcade to hidden parts of the palace.

4

The Hall of the Divan

Four times a week, the imperial council (the **Divan**) met to discuss matters of state and to judge legal cases. The sultan might be present, but more often he would listen through a latticed window high in the wall. Mehmed II rarely attended a meeting of the Divan. He preferred the secret control which the 'dangerous window' gave him.

2

The Gate of Salutation

This gate was the real divide between the outer and the inner worlds of the palace. Only the sultan was allowed to ride a horse through this gate.

5

The Gate of Bliss

Few people ever passed though this gate. The sultan's throne was sometimes placed here at special Muslim festivals.

9
The Imperial Harem
This was the private part of the palace where the Sultan lived with his family. The sultan chose his wives from the many **concubines** in the **harem**. This was the way that the Ottoman sultans produced sons to continue their dynasty.

8
The Chamber of Sacred Relics
This was where the most prized of all the treasures in the Topkapi were kept: the black wool coat of the prophet Muhammad, his standard and footprint. These were brought from Cairo when Egypt fell to the Ottomans.

7
The Throne Room
This was built by Suleyman the Magnificent in 1533. He was the first Sultan to sit on a throne, rather than cross-legged on a carpet. The walls of the Throne Room sparkled with gold and jewels. Foreign ambassadors who were lucky enough to enter the room prostrated themselves three times in front of the sultan. They were then allowed to kiss the hem of his kaftan or the tip of his hanging sleeve.

6
The Third Court
This was a palace within a palace: the 'Abode of Bliss'. It was the silent centre of the sultan's happiness and harmony. To show respect for the sultan no-one was allowed to speak unless invited to do so by the sultan himself. The sultan's pages used sign language and walked on tip-toe. The sultan walked slowly, but everyone else moved at double speed.

Think
- How did the sultan's palace help to make him such a powerful ruler?

STEP 2

Now plan your second programme in the TV series "The Power of the Ottoman Sultans". This programme should explain how the Ottoman Sultans used the Topkapi Palace to show their power.

1 Select five parts of the palace where you think the presenter of the series should be filmed. Explain why you think each of your chosen places should be included in the programme.

2 Imagine two scenes from the palace which could be brought to life using actors. For each scene write a paragraph describing the setting and action.

The Sultan's empire

The Tugra

Think

● How did the Tugra show the power of the sultan?

Do you like practising your signature? When he was a boy, Mehmed II did. He knew that the sultan's special signature, known as the Tugra, was an important symbol of the Ottoman sultans' power. The Tugra was used on all official documents sent from the palace to different parts of the Ottoman Empire. To make the Tugra, early Ottoman leaders simply dipped their thumb and three fingers in ink and pressed them on the page. But look at the Tugra of Suleyman the Magnificent! This Tugra measures about two metres from top to bottom. It is beautifully decorated with flowers and a pattern of intertwining leaves called arabesque.

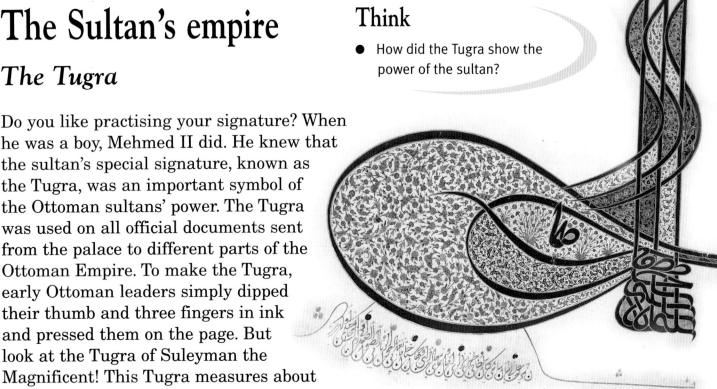

The Tugra of Suleyman the Magnificent

The ruling elite

The Ottoman sultans governed their empire with the help of a ruling elite. These men were all chosen by the sultan. This was very different from Europe where men who were born into the **aristocracy** formed the ruling elite. The most important member of the Ottoman ruling elite was the Grand Vezir. From the time of Mehmed II the Grand Vezir was chosen from among the sultan's slaves.

The Grand Vezir and other members of the ruling elite were made by the sultan. They could be quickly unmade if they displeased

A sixteenth-century picture of the Grand Vezir with visiting ambassadors

the sultan. In the sixteenth century those close to the sultan feared a visit from the sultan's head gardener, for this man was also commander of the imperial guard. When the head gardener and his soldiers appeared carrying a silken cord it meant only one thing: death by strangulation. Ottoman law allowed new sultans to send the silken cord to his living male relatives. This meant that no-one could challenge the power of the sultan.

Think

● How did the Grand Vezir show the power of the sultan?

Taxes, Taxes, Taxes

The Ottoman Empire was a loose empire held together by an efficient **bureaucracy**. This picture shows some of the sultan's bureaucrats working in an office in the Topkapi Palace. There were 25 offices like this one dealing only with the finances of the empire. The efficient Ottoman bureaucracy was an important way in which the sultans showed their power to people living in the Ottoman Empire.

A painting of a public office in the Topkapi Palace

Suleyman the Magnificent ruled over 30 kingdoms and collected taxes from all of them. Every individual in the empire had to pay taxes. Farmers were charged according to the fertility of their soil. Nomads were taxed by the size of their flocks. Jews and Christians within the Ottoman Empire were allowed to practise their faiths, but the Sultan made them pay a special tax. The Sultan's efficient bureaucracy meant that money flowed into his Treasury from every part of his empire.

STEP 3

Now plan your final programme for "The Power of the Ottoman Sultans". This programme should explain how the sultans showed their power through the ways they ruled their empire.

1 Make a list of three main ideas which you think the programme should include. For each idea explain why you think it should form an important part of the programme.

2 Imagine two scenes which could be brought to life using actors. For each scene write a paragraph describing the setting and action.

Thinking your enquiry through

You have probably seen 'trailers' advertising new TV series. Use your plans for each programme to write a script for your presenter to use in the trailer for "The Power of the Ottoman Sultans". He only has one minute, so you will need to think carefully how to capture the viewers' interest. In the trailer there is also time to show three short extracts from your dramatic reconstructions. Which ones will you choose? Make sure you link the script to your chosen reconstructions.

Three Toms' travels

What did English people think about the Islamic world, 1550–1750?

This is the Taj Mahal in Agra, northern India. Many people think that the Taj Mahal is the most perfect building in the world. It was built in the early seventeenth century by the Muslim **Mughal** Emperor, Shah Jahan. The Taj Mahal is a symbol of Shah Jahan's love for his dead wife. It also symbolises the wealth and power of the Mughal Empire.

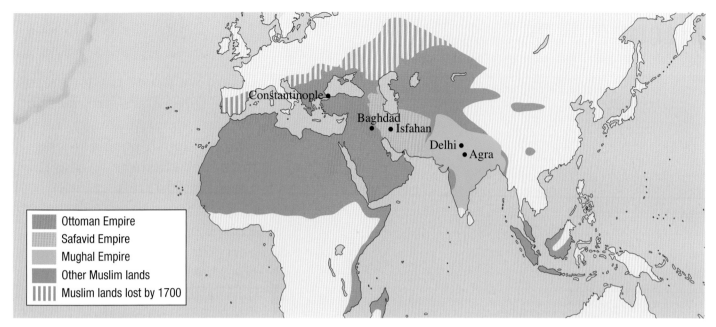

A map of the Islamic world in 1700

In the period 1500–1750, the Mughal Empire was one of three great Islamic empires. As this map shows, the mighty **Ottoman Empire** ruled over a vast area in the west. The **Safavid** Empire, with its capital in Isfahan, covered most of Iran and parts of present-day Iraq. Beyond these empires were other Muslim lands in Africa and Asia.

Think

- What connection do you think people in England might have had with the Islamic world in the period 1550–1750?

Your enquiry

This enquiry is different from the other enquiries in *Meetings of Minds*. Your focus in this final enquiry is not on Muslims themselves, but on English attitudes towards the Islamic world in the period 1550–1750. You will follow the stories of three Englishmen, all called Thomas, who travelled in the Islamic world:

- In 1599, Thomas Dallam sailed to Constantinople to deliver an organ to the Ottoman Sultan;

- In 1612, Thomas Coryate walked all the way to the court of the Mughal Emperor in northern India;

- In 1720, Thomas Pellow, an 11-year-old boy, was captured at sea and became a slave to the **Sultan** of Morocco.

We can find out a lot from these stories about the attitudes of the three Englishmen towards the Muslims. The individual stories also help us to understand the bigger picture of the relationship between England and the Muslim world at that time. At the end of this enquiry you will join some historians as they argue about the best ways of using these stories to find out about English attitudes towards the Islamic world.

Meeting Muslims

Before we follow the journeys of our three Toms, we need to find out about the ways in which English people might have met Muslims during the period 1500–1750.

This is one of the first English portraits of a Muslim. It shows the Moroccan **ambassador** during his visit to London in 1600. The ambassador arrived with a group of 15 officials, merchants and servants. The Moroccans stayed in London for six months and attended many royal celebrations. Queen Elizabeth I was fascinated by Islamic things and entertained many Muslim ambassadors during her reign. She also sent English ambassadors to the courts of Muslim rulers.

Historians can quite easily find out about the visits of Muslim ambassadors by reading official documents and other descriptions. It is harder to find out about contacts between ordinary people. However, historians have discovered that **archives** contain quite a lot of evidence about contacts between English people and Muslims in the period 1550–1750.

A portrait of the Moroccan ambassador, 1600

Think

- How has the artist made the Moroccan ambassador look fierce and stern?

- What might this tell us about English attitudes towards Muslims at that time?

I've found lots of cases of Muslim traders buying and selling goods in England. Charles I even signed a treaty with the ruler of Morocco that allowed Muslim merchants to practise their religion in England. English people living in coastal towns must have met Muslim seamen. There are also many examples of English merchants who traded in Morocco and the Ottoman Empire. Some English traders even went to live in Tangier and Constantinople.

I've discovered many examples of piracy! English and Muslim pirates seem to have raided each others' ships and taken captives. Some Muslim pirates were thrown in jail or put to death in England. There are also hundreds of accounts of English people who were captured by Muslim pirates and then sold in the slave markets of northern Africa.

I'm surprised to find that some English soldiers chose to fight in Muslim armies in the sixteenth and seventeenth centuries. They seem to have mainly fought for the Moroccan and Safavid rulers. The Muslim rulers needed Englishmen who knew about guns and artillery. These English soldiers must have been attracted by the good pay. It's strange to think that Muslim armies included Christian Englishmen.

Think

- What were the main ways in which English people might have met Muslims in the period 1500–1750?

- In what ways did English people have only a limited knowledge of the Muslim world?

Thomas Dallam delivers Queen Elizabeth's organ

In February 1599, Thomas Dallam set sail from England on a six month voyage to Constantinople. Dallam was 26 years old, a talented musician and a skilled craftsman. His big chance came when Queen Elizabeth I learned of the unusual clockwork organ that Dallam had built. The Queen invited Dallam to play the organ at her palace in Whitehall, and was so impressed that she thought it would be an ideal gift to flatter the new Sultan of the Ottoman Empire, Mehmed III. The Queen hoped that Mehmed III would agree to meet her new ambassador in Constantinople, Henry Lello. She also hoped that the new Sultan would continue to allow the English Levant Company to trade with Ottoman ports. Much depended on the success of Dallam's journey.

For Thomas Dallam, the journey to Constantinople in one of Queen Elizabeth's newest and most impressive ships, the *Hector*, was a great adventure. The voyage across the Mediterranean Sea was full of new sights, thrills and dangers. Once the *Hector* reached Ottoman ports, Dallam was able to go ashore. He was fascinated by the houses, clothes and food of the Muslims. In the eastern Mediterranean, Dallam was very impressed by the splendid Ottoman navy. Then, in June, the *Hector* moored close enough to the Turkish coast for Dallam to see the Ottoman army on its way to war. He was not afraid to be so close to the Ottoman army, but the merchants on the *Hector* were too scared to unload any goods in case they were seized by the soldiers.

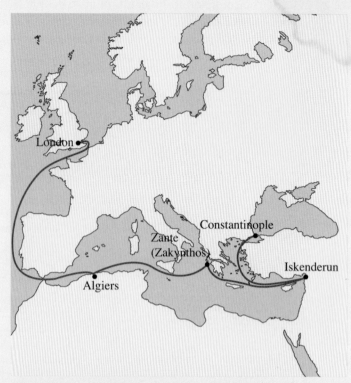

Thomas Dallam's journey to Constantinople

On 16 August, the *Hector* arrived in Constantinople and moored about 3 kilometres away from the Sultan's Topkapi Palace. Mehmed III was very keen to see Queen Elizabeth's fine ship, and the crew of the *Hector* worked hard to repaint their vessel so that it looked its best. The following day, Thomas Dallam took the chests containing the organ to Henry Lello's house. The ambassador had set up a special room so that the organ could be made to look perfect for the Sultan. Dallam could have cried when he opened the chests. After six months in the hold of the ship, Queen Elizabeth's organ had come unstuck! To make matters worse, Henry Lello was very rude about the organ, saying that it was a cheap thing and that it would not impress the Sultan.

Thomas Dallam was determined to prove Lello wrong. For the next 10 days Dallam and his friends repaired the organ. When it was ready, they took it from the English ambassador's house and set it up in the Topkapi Palace. Dallam spent a month in the palace, enjoying the rich furnishings and fine food. On the evening before Dallam was due to play the organ for the Sultan, Henry Lello warned him to be extremely humble and not to expect any reward. It was essential that Mehmed III should like the organ, if Lello was to be allowed to kiss the Sultan's sleeve and the Levant Company was to be granted the right to trade with the Ottomans.

On the morning of 25 September, Dallam was escorted through a series of doors to the Inner Court of the Topkapi Palace. The Sultan ordered silence, and Dallam started his clockwork organ. The Sultan watched in wonder as the clockwork thrushes and blackbirds on top of the organ sang and flapped their wings. He was delighted by Dallam's performance, and rewarded him with 45 pieces of gold. By delighting Mehmed, Thomas Dallam had become the most important Englishman in Constantinople.

But Dallam's success led him into a difficult position. A few days after his performance, he was invited back to the Topkapi Palace where the Sultan's officials tried to persuade him to stay. Dallam was tempted by a life of great luxury in the Sultan's magnificent palace, and by the promise of two wives from the Sultan's **harem**. Lello advised him that it would be dangerous to refuse the Sultan's offer. But, in the end, Thomas Dallam cared too much for his friends, family and country. The following spring, he returned to England.

A portrait of Mehmed III

Think carefully about the story of Thomas Dallam's journey and find as many examples as you can to support the statements of the two historians.

Thomas Dallam's story tells us a lot about his attitudes towards the Muslims.

Yes, his story also helps us to understand a lot about the relationship between England and the Ottoman Empire at that time.

Thomas Coryate walks to the court of the Mughal Emperor

Thomas Coryate was the son of a vicar from Odcombe, in Somerset. He went to Oxford University and became a courtier at the court of James I. Coryate loved to travel and hoped to become famous by writing about his journeys. In 1612, Coryate decided to go on an incredible journey. He planned to walk across the Muslim world to the court of the Mughal Emperor in northern India.

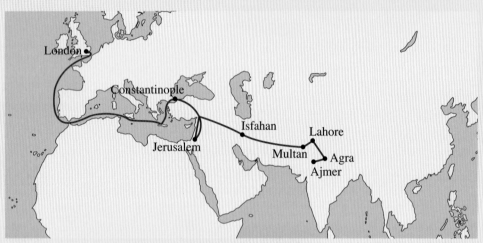

Thomas Coryate's journey to the court of the Mughal Emperor

In October 1612, Coryate set off from England in a small trading ship belonging to the Levant Company. Six months later, he arrived in Constantinople, the capital of the Ottoman Empire. For 10 months, Coryate stayed just outside the city in the comfortable house belonging to James I's ambassador, Paul Pindar. He then left Constantinople and headed for the Holy Land. Coryate walked all the way from Aleppo to Damascus, and then on to Jerusalem. He was a devout Christian and was keen to visit all the sites of the Holy Land. The Christian sites were all under the control of the Ottoman Turks, but Europeans were allowed to visit if they paid a fee. In Jerusalem, Coryate even paid for a tattoo on his left arm. He chose a design of Christian crosses and the words 'the Way, the Truth, the Life' from the Bible.

In September 1614, Coryate began his long and dangerous trek across the barren deserts, great rivers and rugged mountains of Asia to the court of the Mughal Emperor. He travelled in **caravans** with hundreds of camels, horses and people. Coryate walked through the long, hot days, resting by camel-dung fires at night and sleeping under the stars. At Isfahan, the capital of the Safavid Empire, he waited two months for the caravan that would take him all the way to India. On the border between Persia and India, Coryate met another caravan that was travelling west. He was surprised to see Robert Sherley, an English diplomat who was taking gifts (including two elephants and eight antelopes) to the Safavid Emperor.

Some weeks later, Coryate's caravan reached the city of Multan. It was there that Coryate got into an argument about religion with an Italian-speaking Muslim.

Coryate told the man that the Christians were the only true believers. In one of his letters, Coryate wrote: "If I had spoken thus much in Turkey or Persia against Muhammad, they would have roasted me upon a spit; but in the Mughals' dominions, a Christian may speak much more freely than he can in any other Muslim country in the world".

After Coryate's caravan reached its final destination of Lahore, Thomas walked on alone in the heat and dust. He covered 965 kilometres in 30 days, reaching the hill-town of Ajmer in July 1615. This was where he found the court of the Mughal Emperor, Jahangir. To his great delight, it was also where he met a group of English merchants from the East India Company. In the following months, Coryate followed Jahangir's travelling court with his old friend, Sir Thomas Roe. Roe was King James I's ambassador to the Mughal Emperor. He had been sent to secure a trade agreement, which would allow the East India Company to buy a wonderful new cloth called cotton.

Roe and Coryate were given a warm welcome by the Mughal Emperor. Coryate remarked on Jahangir's tolerance towards Christianity and was surprised when the Jahangir spoke of "the great prophet, Jesus". Even when Coryate preached Christianity from the **minaret** of a mosque in Agra, Jahangir took no action. Thomas Coryate planned to spend longer in the Mughal Empire, before walking back to England. But in December 1617 he died of dysentery. Thomas Roe bundled up Coryate's notes of his travels and sent them home to England.

The title page from Thomas Coryate Traveller (1616)

What an amazing journey! Thomas Coryate's story gives us a lot of interesting clues about his attitude towards Muslims.

Yes, and Thomas Coryate's story tells us so much about the relationship between England and the Muslim world in the early seventeenth century.

Think carefully about the story of Thomas Coryate's journey and find as many examples as you can to support the statements of the two historians.

Thomas Pellow becomes a slave to the Sultan of Morocco

In 1715, a trading ship called the *Francis* sailed out of Falmouth harbour. The *Francis* was taking pilchards to Genoa in Italy. On board was Thomas Pellow, an 11-year-old boy who was going to sea for the first time. Thomas had persuaded his parents to let him leave school and become a sailor on his uncle's ship. He hoped to return in six months' time. In fact, it would be 23 years before Thomas Pellow returned to England. Within two years of his return to England, Pellow had published a book full of colourful stories about his adventures.

This was a dangerous time to be at sea. For many years, northern African pirates, known as the **Barbary corsairs**, had terrorised European ships. The Barbary corsairs had even attacked coastal villages in southwest England, capturing men, women and children, and selling them at slave markets in northern Africa. The man who bought most of these European slaves was the Sultan of Morocco, Moulay Ismail. The Sultan knew that by capturing large numbers of Christian slaves, he could increase his power over European monarchs. In 1714, he had released some of his English slaves in return for presents of chinaware, cloth and 12 spotted deer. But, a year later, the presents had still not arrived. At the same time as the *Francis* set sail, Moulay Ismail ordered his corsairs back to sea.

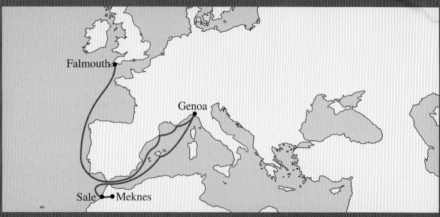

Thomas Pellow's journey to Meknes

According to Pellow's book, it was on the return journey from Genoa that the crew of the *Francis* faced an attack by the Barbary corsairs. Pellow writes that he was terrified as the corsairs, with their shaved heads and flashing scimitars, climbed on-board the *Francis*. The corsairs separated Thomas from his uncle, placed him in shackles and took him to the Moroccan coastal town of Salè. After four days of misery in Salè's underground slave pens, Thomas Pellow and 52 other English captives were made to walk 190 kilometres to Meknes, the Moroccan capital. Here they were handed over to their new owner, Moulay Ismail.

Most of Moulay Ismail's European slaves worked for 15 hours a day, building the Sultan's huge new palace in Meknes. However, the Sultan decided to give Thomas Pellow to one of his favourite sons, Moulay es-Sfa. In his book, Pellow fills this part of his story with vivid and shocking details. He tells us how, at first, Moulay es-Sfa tried to persuade Thomas to convert to Islam, but, when Thomas refused, Moulay es-Sfa began to beat him and to deny him food for days on end. After months of torture, Thomas broke down and agreed to become a Muslim.

News of Pellow's conversion reached Moulay Ismail, and the Sultan decided that

Thomas Pellow should now be trained as one of his personal slaves. Thomas worked in the palace garden, then as a guard in the Sultan's harem and, finally, as one of Moulay Ismail's personal attendants. Pellow was now 16, and the Sultan decided that he should marry. His bride came from an important Moroccan family. The family organised a wedding feast and treated Thomas generously. It was not long before Thomas Pellow's wife gave birth to a baby daughter. His Muslim wife and child gave Thomas much happiness in the years that followed.

In 1720, Thomas Pellow became a slave-soldier in the Sultan's army. He was pleased to leave behind the Sultan's palace, but his life as a soldier was difficult and dangerous. He longed to return to England and even dreamed about taking his wife and child with him. Then one day, 10 years after his marriage, a messenger brought him dreadful news: both his wife and daughter had died. Thomas was distraught. He longed even more to return to England.

On a moonless spring night in 1737, Thomas Pellow crept out of his Meknes barracks and slipped through the gates of the city. His fluent Arabic, long beard and tanned skin enabled him to pass himself off as a wandering Arab merchant. After several months on the road, Pellow reached the Atlantic port of Willadia. There he persuaded an Irish sea captain to take him back to England. Thomas prepared to return to his own country for the first time in 23 years. Once home, he began to write the story of his travels – a story that many English people would read.

A portrait of Moulay Ismail

93

Think carefully about the story of Thomas Pellow's journey and find as many examples as you can to support the statements of the two historians.

I find Thomas Pellow's attitude towards Muslims very interesting.

I'm fascinated by what Thomas Pellow's story might tell us about the relationship between England and the Muslim world in the early eighteenth century.

Thinking your enquiry through

The historians are beginning to have a rather heated discussion. Which of the views do you agree with and why?

But you're missing the point! Even if they are not totally true, the stories Pellow told in his book must have shaped English ideas about Muslims. His book is useful because it helps us to understand how English attitudes might have been formed.

Wait a minute! I'm not sure we should trust Pellow. Parts of his account must have been exaggerated so that people would buy his book. For example, he probably made out Moulay Ismail to be much more cruel than he was.

Well, I don't think we should be studying a story about an English slave in Morocco at all. Surely it's more important to study all the positive encounters between English people and Muslims.

So are you saying that we should just ignore English people's fear of the Barbary corsairs? That's not good history! We need to know more about all the different encounters between English people and Muslims at that time – good and bad.

Glossary

Abbasids — Caliphs over the Muslim world (750–1258)

Abyssinian Empire — Christian empire that was based in what we now call Ethiopia

Allah — The Arab name for God

alliance — Partnership between countries

ambassador — Person who represents his nation in a foreign country

archives — A collection of historical documents

aristocracy — Nobles e.g. dukes and earls

Barbary corsairs — Pirates from north Africa

bedouins — Tribes that live in the deserts of Arabia

berber — A group of tribes from north west Africa

biased — Showing bias. Accidentally or deliberately being one-sided, not being fair to all sides

bureaucracy — Work done by government officials (bureaucrats)

Byzantine Empire — Eastern half of the Roman Empire. From c. 325 AD it was a Christian empire

Caliph — Leader of the Muslim community after Muhammad's death

caravan — Group of travellers, e.g. on camels

caravansary — An inn where traders and their animals would rest

Carthaginians — North Africans who ruled parts of Spain c. 300 BC

chivalry — Rules of noble behaviour

clan — Group of families

concubine — A mistress, an unmarried woman living with a man

cowrie shell — Small shells used as money in parts of Africa and Asia

crusade — War by Christians to regain control of lands lost to non-Christians

divan — A group of advisers

Emir — Governor or prince

empire — A group of countries ruled by one person

Franks — Name given by Muslims to Christians from north and west Europe

Hajj — Muslim pilgrimage to Makkah

Hanifs — Arabs who believed there was only one God, even before Islam taught this

harem — Private living area of a powerful Muslim man and his wives, concubines and family e.g. the Ottoman Emperor

Hejira — The event when Muhammad escaped from Makkah in 622. This became Year 1 in the Muslim dating system

idol — An image or object worshipped as a god

infidels — Unbelievers e.g. used by Muslims to describe Christians and by Christians to describe Muslims

Islam — The name of the Muslim religion. It means 'Surrender to God's will'.

Jihad — Name given by Muslims for war against enemies of Islam. It can also mean an inner struggle to be holy

jinn — Supernatural beings or spirits

Kaaba — Muslim shrine at Makkah. Small black building holding a sacred stone.

liberators — People who set others free

madrasas	Colleges where Islamic subjects e.g. law are taught
Mamluks	Soldiers brought from Turkey to serve as slaves in the Egyptian army. In 1250 they took control and ruled Egypt until 1811
mihrab	An opening in a wall found inside a mosque. Muslims face the mihrab to pray
minaret	Slender tower attached to a mosque from which Muslims are called to prayer
Mongols	Tribe from central Asia that conquered huge areas from China to eastern Europe c. 1200–1400
Moors	Name often given to Muslims who settled in Spain
mosque	Building used for worship by Muslims
Muslim	Person who follows religion of Islam and the teaching of the prophet Muhammad
Mughal	Powerful Muslim family whose empire in India lasted from 1526 to 1857
nomad	Member of a tribe that has no permanent home
Ottomans	Turkish family who ruled a powerful Muslim Empire from c. 1300 to 1920. At its peak it controlled lands in eastern Europe as well as the middle east
pagan	Person who believes in many gods
Persia	Country now called Iran
pilgrim	Person who goes on a journey (pilgrimage) to a holy place
Quraysh	Arab tribe that ruled Mecca when Muhammad was born
Quran	The holy book of Islam. Muslims believe this is the word of God revealed to Muhammad

revelation	A message revealed by God
Safavid	Powerful Muslim family whose empire in Persia (modern Iran) lasted from 1501 to 1726
saracens	Name given by northern Europeans to Muslims in the Middle Ages
Sasanian Empire	Powerful empire that ruled much of the Middle East when Muhammad was born. Based in modern Iran
Seljuk	A tribe of Muslim Turks that moved into the area we now call Turkey c. 1070
Shi'ites	Smaller of the two main groups in Islam. Shi'a Muslims believe caliphs should be from Muhammad's family. (See also Sunni)
successor	Someone who takes over from another person
Sufi	Type of Muslim who seeks a direct experience of God
Sultan	Islamic title for a ruler over Muslim lands
Sunnis	Largest group of Muslims. Believe the caliph did not need to be a member of Muhammad's family, but should be whichever man was most likely to keep the traditions of Muhammad. (See also Shi'ites)
Turks	Tribes from central Asia. Some moved west to settle in the land we now call Turkey
Umayyads	The clan that ruled the Muslim world as caliphs, 661 to 750
Visigoths	Tribe from eastern Europe that invaded the Roman Empire and ruled Spain from c. 500 to 711